T0248204

FRONT★LINE LEADERSHIP

PATRICK NELSON

FRONT★LINE LEADERSHIP

HOW TO ELIMINATE COMPLACENCY AND BUILD ALL-IN ENGAGEMENT

WILEY

Published by John Wiley & Sons, Inc., Hoboken, New Jersey.
Published simultaneously in Canada.

For general information on our other products and services or for technical support, please contact our Customer Care Department within the United States at (800) 762-2974, outside the United States at (317) 572-3993 or fax (317) 572-4002.

Wiley also publishes its books in a variety of electronic formats. Some content that appears in print may not be available in electronic formats. For more information about Wiley products, visit our web site at www.wiley.com.

Library of Congress Cataloging-in-Publication Data:

Names: Nelson, Patrick, author.
Title: Front-line leadership : how to eliminate complacency and build
  all-in engagement / Patrick Nelson.
Description: Hoboken, New Jersey : Wiley, [2024] | Includes index.
Identifiers: LCCN 2024014087 (print) | LCCN 2024014088 (ebook) | ISBN
  9781394240753 (hardback) | ISBN 9781394240777 (adobe pdf) | ISBN
  9781394240760 (epub)
Subjects: LCSH: Leadership.
Classification: LCC HD57.7 .N463 2024 (print) | LCC HD57.7 (ebook) | DDC
  658.4/092—dc23/eng/20240416
LC record available at https://lccn.loc.gov/2024014087
LC ebook record available at https://lccn.loc.gov/2024014088

Cover Design: Wiley
Author Photo: Courtesy of the Author

SKY10075475_051824

For Shanna and my four Hs—you are my everything.

Contents

Introduction

When I was growing up, most people did not look at me and think "Man, that kid is going places!" Except maybe to jail. Thankfully, some people saw potential in me and encouraged me to do better and to be better. They helped transform me from being one of the last people you would associate with the idea of leadership to someone who is now helping entire organizations successfully transform their leadership culture. In this book I want to share the lessons of how I grew my leadership skills and how you can grow yours, too. To take that journey together, let's go back and start at the beginning.

I grew up in a small town in rural Minnesota. And when I say "small town," I mean no stop lights, no movie theater, no McDonalds. If you were driving through and blinked, you might miss the town altogether. I certainly was not born with a silver spoon in my mouth. By the time I was 12 years old, I had lived in seven different trailers/apartments/houses, often having to share a small room with my three brothers. It wasn't great, but it could have been worse. My mother and my stepfather both worked to provide for us, but they didn't make much money, and we often went without.

I enlisted in the active Army soon after high school, and this is where I cultivated my core leadership skills and behaviors. I went on to serve for nearly 7 years (6 years, 10 months, and 22 days, but who's counting?) as a paratrooper in the historic 173rd Airborne Brigade based out of Vicenza, Italy. I deployed a total of three times between Iraq and Afghanistan for a total of 39 months in combat.

As I was finishing my military service, I went to college and earned two master's degrees while also embarking on a journey that ultimately led to my career as a leadership consultant and speaker.

I have been shaped into the leader that I am today by the sum of all of my experiences, my successes, and especially my failures—I'm a big believer in learning from your mistakes. In this book I will share with you the lessons that I have learned through my stories, many of which still feel like they happened yesterday. The sounds, the smells, the taste—they are as vivid now as they ever were.

I also would not be here today without those who believed in me. From a difficult childhood, to serving in the Army and being wounded in combat, to battling addiction and trying to find a purpose in life, many people have impacted me greatly. It is an honor to share their legacies with you.

Being a Leader

As someone who cut their teeth in one of the best leadership laboratories in the world, the United States Army, I firmly believe that you do not need to be the boss or be in charge of people to be a leader. The military is one of the most bureaucratic organizations out there. We would wear our rank on our uniform every single day, and everyone knew exactly where they stood in the hierarchy of command. Yet you could still find leaders at even the lowest levels, and they were not in charge of anything. They embraced the military definition of a leader, which is not about your rank or title. It's someone who inspires others and influences outcomes, which is known as front-line leadership.

Now in the civilian world, I enjoy leading leadership development workshops, and one exercise I like to do is to have team members design a perfect leader (as if one ever existed). Take a minute to think about what qualities you want in a leader. I imagine it includes things such as being a good listener, having empathy, motivating people, holding themselves accountable, leading by example, being credible, and so on. I've yet to see someone describe their perfect leader as being the boss or being in charge of people. And the reason people don't name those things is because leadership is about the behaviors that a person demonstrates. You do not need to be the official boss to be a good listener, and you don't need to be in charge of people to lead by example. You could be a new employee at your first job and be one of the most empathetic people in your organization. I firmly believe anyone can develop leadership skills and behaviors with the right knowledge and experience.

Using This Book

This book is written for leaders at all levels, from the future leaders who feel a stirring inside of them to make things better but are not sure what to do, to those who have led teams and organizations for years and are looking for inspirational and practical ways to continue to engage their people.

In these pages, I will take you on a journey through some of my greatest failures, challenges, and ultimately successes in both the military and civilian worlds. These are augmented by lessons from working closely with a wide range of organizations in helping them shift their cultures. These experiences have helped me develop a leadership philosophy that is positive, practical, and actionable. Best of all, anyone can use it to become a better leader.

This book is organized in three main parts:

- Part I: Leading Yourself
- Part II: Leading the Team
- Part III: Leading the Culture

If you expect others to follow you, you obviously need to be able to lead yourself first. This first part of the book will give you practical tips that will help you increase your self-awareness, embrace a growth mindset, learn how to more effectively manage your emotions during times of stress and change, and how to persevere better through adversity.

The second part of the book will examine ways in which you can help better lead teams. You'll learn how to help meet the needs of others, lead by example, motivate your team, and delegate in a way that promotes trust and growth.

The third part of the book provides stories, tips, and techniques for shaping organizational culture. These chapters will focus on developing a culture of accountability, the importance and ways in which we recognize and reward people, and how we can take all of this to truly empower our people to do great things.

My hope is that you find inspiration in these pages through the challenges that I have faced and overcome. However, that inspiration cannot just live in the moment. Please take the practical tips that I share to help you navigate your own challenges. I would love to hear how they help you, so please don't hesitate to reach out to me at patrick@loyaltypointleadership.com.

Leading Yourself

Leading yourself is a profound journey of self-awareness, discipline, and continuous growth. In this first part of the book, we're going to explore key topics that serve as building blocks for enhancing your leadership skills and propelling you to new levels of effectiveness. By delving into these foundational aspects, you'll gain valuable insights that contribute to your development as a more adept and impactful leader.

1

Discover and Ignite Your Purpose

Everyone's lives changed on the Tuesday morning of September 11, 2001. Whether you were getting ready for school, at the office, or not even born yet, the world was never going to be the same after that day. The innocence of years past was shattered as we watched the tragedy unfold live on television. This became a defining moment for many of us—a moment that helped me discover and ignite my purpose.

On September 11, 2001, I was in the third week of my first semester at a small community college in rural Minnesota. I didn't have the type of family that encouraged me to go to college. They didn't take me on college visits, help me fill out applications, or submit financial aid forms. I had to do it all myself. I had barely graduated high school, and with no real direction in life, I started skipping classes that very first week. As far as college was concerned, I wasn't on the fast track to success.

As I watched the events of 9/11 unfold on the television before me, I felt those same feelings that most of us felt—helplessness, sorrow, and anger. I knew I had to do something. I couldn't just sit idly by as our country was getting ready to go to war with those responsible.

I visited the Army recruiter's office the day after the attack, but they were closed. I came back the next day and told them that I wanted to enlist in the active Army. At that time I was a member of the Minnesota National Guard, but I knew the National Guard would not be the first ones called up, if at all. Little did I know that the prolonged Global War on Terror would see numerous National Guard units deploy multiple times to combat zones and many National Guard soldiers pay the ultimate sacrifice. The challenges that I faced as a child helped fuel my desire to achieve more in life and I think even gave me a leg up on others as I began my active-duty military career.

Purpose Is Your Journey, Not Your Job

I was only 18 when that defining moment happened that set me on a journey driven by purpose. But that journey has been filled with many ups and downs, twists and turns—many times where I had to rediscover and shift my purpose as I grew older. Though the stories I share in this chapter will be different than your specific situation, the principles I outline still apply, and when put into practice they can help you discover and ignite your purpose.

When I think of purpose, I think of the sense of having meaning and fulfillment, the idea that what I do in life—whether it's my personal life or professional life—is bringing me joy and making a difference. That purpose is different for everyone. Does that mean that your day-to-day job is always going to define what your purpose is? Of course not. One of my best friends since I was a kid, Bruce Koepp, works full-time at the local soybean processing plant in our small town in rural Minnesota. He likes his job, but that doesn't mean it defines who he is and or what his bigger purpose is. He knows that it is part of the process. You see, Bruce's purpose is farming. He loves it. But farming is tough and his full-time job allows him the benefits he needs to support his family while also pursuing his passion.

Proactively Pursuing Opportunities

Do you ever feel stuck? Like you're just going through the motions day in and day out? You don't have to. You can change that. 9/11 was obviously a big event, one that served as a call to action for many. I pray we never have another event like that. Your opportunity to break out of the rut may not play out on television like mine did; it may not knock on your door or ring on the phone. More than likely, you need to be proactive, willing to take a chance to step outside of your comfort zone and take a risk doing something different. That idea was put to the test early on in my military career.

In January of 2002 I was stationed in Bamberg, Germany, with the headquarters unit of an artillery brigade. This unit had Multiple Launch Rocket Systems, rather than the type of job that the Army had specifically trained me for: shooting howitzer cannons. Since they didn't have my particular job, they assigned me to be the colonel's driver. I didn't drop out of college after 9/11 to drive a colonel around and make sure his coffee was hot. I signed up because I wanted to be part of the fight.

Early in the summer of 2002, our unit was conducting a two-week training rotation to a place called Grafenwoehr in Germany. As I finished unloading some of my stuff from the Humvee, I looked up in the sky as I heard the unmistakable "whoop-whoop" of the double rotor blades of a Chinook helicopter passing overhead. I watched as, one by one soldiers, jumped out of the back and their parachutes opened. At that moment, I knew that was what I wanted to do. My first sergeant, George Harvey, happened to be standing next to me. He knew that I would rather be doing something else besides driving the colonel. Later on that evening he did something very uncommon—he took me to where this unit was staying and introduced me to some of their leadership, telling them that I wanted to join them. I never saw or heard that happen again throughout my nearly seven years in the Army.

As a young private first class in the Army, you can't just say you don't like your job and ask for another one. You are there for the needs of the Army. Where they tell you to go, you go. But that moment standing there, watching these high-speed soldiers parachute to the ground, stirred something inside of me. A few weeks later, my first sergeant called me into his office and recommended that I try to get what is known as a letter of acceptance from some of the senior leadership in that airborne unit. With his connections and my tenacity, I secured letters from Command Sergeant Major Wade Gunther—the top enlisted soldier in the 173rd Airborne Brigade based in Vicenza, Italy. I also received one from the command sergeant major of the Southern European Task Force, which the 173rd fell under.

There was a lot of back and forth on the phone and through email over the next month with people from the Army personnel command. At that time, there was only one Field Artillery Battery in the 173rd Airborne Brigade—Delta Battery (The Doghouse) of the 319th Field Artillery Regiment. So out of roughly 2,500 soldiers in the brigade, only about 120 were Field Artillery. You need to either be lucky and/or know someone to get assigned to that unit. I think I had a little bit of both on my side as I officially got reassigned to the 173rd Airborne Brigade in August of 2002.

Take a moment and think about your career. Most of us have probably taken a job with an organization with the hopes of moving up the ranks in that company. But depending on the size of the company and the industry, moving up might require you to have a breadth of experience. What are you doing to seek out those experiences? Are you actively pursuing them or just waiting for someone to ask one day? I knew that I wanted to do something unique in my military career and I was not satisfied with my initial role. We will always have some type of constraints on us—financial, time, geographical, family, the list goes on. I found a way to work within the constraints of the military by getting letters of acceptance. Trust me, if I can do that as a private first class in the Army, I know you can do it too.

What might that actually look like for you? Maybe you have a strong desire to work in marketing, but you took that open job in HR to get your foot in the door. Are you networking with those who are currently working in marketing? Does your manager and their manager know your desire? Have you sought opportunities to potentially partner on projects with marketing? You also need to be performing in your current role if you want them to help you pursue your professional goal.

Committing to Your Path

I would be lying If I said it was easy showing up to a new unit full of paratroopers who proudly wore their jump wings on their uniform, and I had nothing. Let's just say they did not let me forget that I was still a dirty nasty leg (a term of endearment paratroopers have for those not airborne qualified). Serving in the military can be very physically demanding but they do a really good job of getting you in shape. I really didn't find it all that difficult to find success and move up in the ranks early in my career. My new first sergeant, James Mitchell, gave me some great advice: "If you want to be successful in this Army, all you have to do are three things: do what you're told, do what you're told, do what you're damn well told." For the most part, it worked out pretty good for me.

I mentioned how the Army does a good job of getting you in shape, but I was definitely not prepared for the demanding physicality of being a paratrooper, which was quite different than the unit I was in previously. This was evident in the very first run

I did with my new unit. In my old unit, I used to run with what was known as the "A Group," which consisted of the fastest runners in the unit. When the time came early in the morning to get into groups to run at my new unit, I bravely lined up with the "A Group." It was not pretty. That was the only time I have ever fallen out of a run—when you're not able to keep up with the rest—and it was very humbling.

In February of 2003, I was sent to Fort Benning, Georgia, for airborne school. At that time, there was a lot of talk of an imminent war in Iraq. As much as I wanted to go to airborne school, I was afraid I would miss the war—my chance to actually do something. Airborne school is three weeks long. It's been said that after the first week, they separate the boys and girls from the men and the women. After the second week, they separate the men and the women from the fools. The third week, the fools jump out of the airplanes. I successfully completed airborne school and earned my wings in early March and went straight back to Italy to join my unit. They were getting everything ready to head to Iraq once we received the word. I was excited and scared.

I ended up deploying a total of three times during my military career: once to Iraq beginning during the initial invasion for 12 months, once to Afghanistan for 12 months, and back to Afghanistan again on my last deployment for 15 months. I had reenlisted twice to stay in the Army and specifically to stay with the same unit. I didn't want to go anywhere else. I wanted to be in a unit that was going to be on the front lines on the Global War on Terrorism. And the 173rd Airborne Brigade was the tip of the spear.

The last deployment to Afghanistan was challenging, to say the least. We jokingly called our platoon the most versatile platoon in the Army, and I don't think we were far off with that assessment. We were artillerymen by trade but with this being my third deployment, I had only done that job for about half of the time. The other half was conducting missions normally reserved for our infantry brothers. On this last deployment, our mission changed drastically three different times.

We started out conducting force protection operations at a small Combat Outpost (COP) in northeast Afghanistan, in the Nuristan province. This location would later be made infamous in the movie *The Outpost*, which depicted the final battle at the COP on October 3, 2009, in which 8 American soldiers were killed and 27 were wounded. Two brave men were awarded the Medal of Honor for their courage that day, Clint Romesha and Ty Carter. Tactically, it was a terrible location to be at. We were surrounded on all sides by towering mountains. We were the proverbial fish in the barrel.

We spent May to August of 2007 at COP Keating, and then our platoon was tasked with dusting off our howitzer cannons and heading south for a more traditional artillery-type mission supporting ground operations and conducting counterfire operations. In January of 2008, we were once again tasked with a different mission—conducting border control operations at the Torkham Gate, the highest-trafficked legal border crossing between Afghanistan and Pakistan.

Changing Your Course

All good things must come to an end, or so I've heard. I had a decision to make during my last deployment to Afghanistan. Should I reenlist for another couple of years? Should I make a career out of the Army? The three back-to-back-to-back deployments had taken a toll on me mentally and physically. During my last deployment, the Army had put me on orders to go train new lieutenants in Fort Sill, Oklahoma, at the Officers Basic Course (OBC). OBC is designed for newly commissioned officers fresh out of college to prepare them for service in the Army. Now, nothing against lieutenants or the great state of Oklahoma, but I had zero desire to do that. I knew that if I was going to be in the Army, I needed to be in a front-line unit like the 173rd Airborne Brigade.

I had seen many soldiers leave the Army with high aspirations to go to college or start a business when they got out. But from my experience, many of them didn't have much of a plan in place. They had a dream, but they weren't taking any steps to help get them in the right direction. When I made the decision to leave the Army, I knew that I was going to go back to college and finish my bachelor's degree. It was a goal that I had ever since I was in elementary school. But I also knew that if I waited and didn't start right away, I probably wouldn't do it. I've seen it happen to many people. On my R&R trip back to the States from Afghanistan, I started to put the wheels in motion. I needed a vehicle, and I needed a place to live.

I honestly didn't put a lot of thought into where I was going to go to college—I just knew that I wanted to be close to Shanna, the beautiful girl I had met while I was back home right before my last deployment. She was playing basketball at a small private college in Mankato, Minnesota. There was a four-year state college in that town—Minnesota State University, Mankato—and I figured that would work for me. During that last time back home, I bought a car, and I signed a lease for an apartment in a small town near Mankato. Now I just needed to figure out how to get accepted into college while I was busy in Afghanistan conducting combat operations.

When you change course while pursuing your purpose, you need to make sure you're networking with the right people. I found LinkedIn and other social media apps to be great tools to help connect with me those who were doing what I wanted to do. I started to connect with former military members who had left the Army and started going to school. I sent them messages and asked for their advice. You need to be proactive.

I started to fill out the online application for Minnesota State, but I got to the part where they needed a copy of all my previous college transcripts—including from that initial very brief moment in time prior to 9/11. At that time, the previous school that I attended did not have a way for me to request my transcripts online. I could mail something to them, but I really didn't put a lot of trust in the mail system in Afghanistan. So I gave them a call.

I explained to the person on the phone that I needed an official copy of my transcript sent over to Minnesota State. She said that would be no problem; I could come by and pick it up anytime. It was at that moment that I realized I had failed to mention that I was calling from Afghanistan. After a short laugh, she said she could bend the procedures a little bit and help me out. Awesome— everything was on track.

That is, until a few weeks later, when I was devastated to get an email saying that my application was not accepted into school because my official transcript from my previous stint in community college showed that I received two Fs. But that couldn't be right. I had withdrawn from all my classes; I dropped out to join the Army! I called that community college back and I was told that there was no way they could change an official grade; it could only be done by the teacher who gave the grade. I pleaded my case—why would I only drop out of three of my classes when I was joining the Army? There had to have been some mistake.

But I wasn't going to let this small hurdle stand in the way of plans. Thankfully, there was an appeals process I could use to challenge the decision. I had to write a 1,000-word essay to the admissions board on why my acceptance in to school would be a good decision. This provided me with the platform to explain the situation and the two Fs that were on my official transcript. But I thought about it for a moment—I didn't like hearing excuses from my soldiers on why they came up short. I wanted solutions and I bet this admissions board wanted the same. So I focused my essay on the future and the value that I could provide to the university and to other students with my experiences. A week later, I was accepted! Not only that, but I applied for a Horatio Alger Military Scholarship and was honored to be selected.

What's your reaction when obstacles get in your way? Do you make excuses that hold you back? It probably depends on what the consequences are. If Minnesota State was not going to accept me, I knew most others also would not because their admissions criteria were similar. I was set on going to college and I was not going to let some administrative issue prevent that from happening.

I was never a great student but I ended up getting As in every college class I took (setting aside those two previous Fs, of course), except for three Bs—from a double major in history and sport management, to a master's degree in sport management, and a master's degree in organization development. How did I do that? It was definitely not because I have a high IQ. I applied the same advice that my first sergeant told me a long time ago: "Do what you're told, do what you're told, do what you're damn well told." It's amazing what happens in school when you actually do the readings that are assigned and you actually apply yourself. I was sitting in a college classroom with a bunch of 18- and 19-year-old kids. Their biggest worry was where the party was happening and who was going to buy the beer. I was 26 at the time and much more focused. College can be a great social experience for many people, but I was not there for that. I was there to do the best that I could and to graduate.

I wish I could shout this from the rooftops with a bull horn: you don't need to go to college to be successful or to discover or ignite your purpose. Everyone's path is different. Is there a cause you are passionate about? Feeding the homeless, helping the elderly, supporting veterans, animal rescue? What are you doing to feed that passion? You need to be seeking opportunities that bring you joy. You need to pick up the phone, hop on Google, meet with people. You need to be active, otherwise your only valid excuse is yourself.

Handling Adversity While Finding Your Purpose

Like many people, I had a difficult childhood. I give a lot of credit for breaking free from that to a mentor I had through a program called Big Buddy. This program matched young kids from challenging backgrounds with young adults (usually college students) to mentor them. I was matched up with a young college student named Brad Delano. Brad was awesome. He was everything that I had wanted out of a dad: someone who would play catch with me, ask me how my day was going, even throw me a birthday party. Brad helped show me that there was more to life, that I was not destined to follow in the footsteps of family members before me.

When I left the Army, I went to school and I went home. I began to isolate myself. I knew that was a dangerous path. I found the local version of the Big Buddy program—Big Brothers at the local YMCA. I filled out all the necessary paperwork and background checks and was soon matched with a young man named Isaiah. I related a lot to Isaiah. He was one of three boys raised by a single mother. Besides being able to work with Isaiah, I also volunteered every week on Friday nights where those kids who were not matched with a Big Brother would be invited to the YMCA for food and fun. It was awesome. I definitely got just as much out of it as the kids did, if not more.

School was the easy part for me—it was everything else that was hard. We've all heard of the challenges military men and women face when they transition to the civilian world, but I thought I was going to be immune to that. I was stronger than that. Nope. Wrong. Physically, I was in a lot of pain from the wounds I sustained in Afghanistan. What I thought was just one small piece of shrapnel still in my back ended up being several pieces. The doctor at the Veterans Affairs (VA) hospital showed me the X-ray and I couldn't believe it. For me, it was a psychological problem more than anything else—knowing that I had pieces of what the enemy used to kill and hurt my friends with me every day. The doctors told me that scar tissue had formed around the pieces, which is your body's way of protecting you. Well, those hard balls of scar tissues are embedded in muscle along my back and cause a lot of pain.

There wasn't any plan to help make the pain go away permanently but the VA offered me pain pills and I gladly accepted. Besides helping to dull the pain, I liked how they made feel at first—or more accurately, how they helped me not feel. They helped me forget about the challenges of my past and my failures. And the loss of my friends.

During those first two years after the Army, I also had two surgeries to fix my shoulder and I became addicted to pain pills. I didn't go anywhere without a few pills in my pocket that I could pop at a moment's notice. Of course, the pills didn't make my problems go away. They only made them worse. They served as accelerants for the challenges that I was already facing.

But thankfully, after five years of taking them, I finally broke free from the addiction thanks to the support from Shanna and some innovative therapy that a veterans organization hooked me up with. I don't think I would still be alive if I had not kicked that addiction. Breaking the chains of addiction truly allowed me the opportunity to focus and seek a new purpose in life.

Once thing I know to be true is that we all have adversity in our lives, and it looks different for everyone. And that's okay! Not everyone is going to have traumatic childhoods, addiction challenges, or get shot at in war. It could be a job loss, workplace conflicts, financial hardships, or myriad other challenges that we face in our journey. The principles that have helped me discover and ignite my purpose can also help you do the same. But here's the hard part—it's now on you. My promise to you is that if you take some of these tips that I share with you, you will be well on your way.

Your Challenge

Discovering your purpose is a very personal journey that requires some self-reflection and some honest assessment of where you are in your life.

1. Make a list of things in life that bring you joy.
2. Make a list of things that you are currently good at.
3. Make a list of things that make you feel good about yourself.
4. Look for connection points between these three lists, and draw lines connecting them if you need to. What themes emerged? Explore those connections and learn more. Talk to people who are doing those things, ask them questions, and remain curious.

Whether it's potential volunteer opportunities to pursue your passion or finding a job that connects to your passion, visualize your success.

2

Embracing a Growth Mindset

I like to think of myself as a little bit of a leadership geek. I love digging into the research behind leadership—the stats, the data, the experiments—all of it. When I speak and when I write, I don't just like to say stuff because it sounds good, I need something to back it up. And one of the first pieces of research that I stumbled upon was from Carol Dweck, a brilliant professor at Stanford who has pioneered the research behind the concept of a growth mindset.

Dweck has done extensive research on motivation and achievement, and one specific study really captured my attention. The researchers would put a kid in a room and give them a puzzle to complete. The first one was easy. Once that puzzle was completed, they would receive another puzzle that was a little more difficult. That process continued—as they completed each puzzle, they were given one that was a little more difficult. What the researchers found was that those with fixed mindsets were much more likely to give up and end the study. Those who had a growth mindset actually became more and more exhilarated as the puzzles became more and more challenging. They thrived on the idea that they might come up short but that it would be a huge learning opportunity for them.

People who have a fixed mindset like to stay in what I call their "nookie-blankie" zone. This is the stuff that they know how to do and they don't want to try anything else for fear of failure. A fixed mindset can show up in numerous ways in our lives. It doesn't have to be the stereotypical idea of getting an F on a test. It could be our resistance to receiving critical feedback or our emotionally driven reaction to a change at work or how we compare ourselves to others.

On the other hand, those with a growth mindset see risks as opportunities. They don't let failure define who they are, and they view these opportunities as chances to learn, grow, and get better at something.

Understanding Your Own Expectations

As I studied Professor Dweck's research, I began to reflect on moments in my life when I've faced adversity and failure. In the previous chapter, I mentioned the challenges I had showing up to a unit full of paratroopers when I was not yet airborne qualified. I failed to mention that these guys were also really good at their jobs, the best of the best when it comes to field artillery. In field artillery, and specifically as a cannon crewmember on a towed M119 howitzer cannon, there is a position known as a gunner. The gunner is usually the second in command behind the section chief. The gunner is responsible for inputting the data sent by the fire direction center on to the gunner's sight and traversing and elevating the cannon tube to the specific spot to fire the round at the target.

Now, when I say inputting data, this is all done manually—no computers involved. For example, a fire mission may be announced over the radio. The gunner needs to listen for the deflection and quadrant to put on their gunner's sight. This involves turning two knobs to these numbers, but it needs to be precise. (You cannot simply inch back the knob if you pass the deflection number—you need to wind the knob back and try again not to strip the gears.) Once this is done, the gunner then needs to look through their sight at a device called a collimator, which is like a small telescope with numbers. The gunner must turn the traversing wheel to line up the numbers in their sight picture to those on the collimator while at the same time turning the elevation wheel and leveling the two bubbles on the site mount. While the gunner is doing all of this, the other members of the crew are preparing the artillery round, potentially setting the timed fuse, and loading it. The skill required to be a good gunner is difficult—and it's also a perishable skill—which means you need to continue to practice if you want to be good.

The first time I saw a gunner doing this—turning and burning on the gunner's sight—I was blown away. I was very intimidated and proclaimed that I never wanted to be a gunner. It just looked way too difficult. I didn't care if it would impact my career or my ability to move up in rank; I wanted nothing to do with it. I was 100% stuck in a fixed mindset. But thankfully I had some great leadership who saw through that and even commented that they've been in my shoes and know how intimidating it can look. So what did they do? They invested their time to train me and to teach me. And I took advantage of every opportunity I had to do that. Eventually, I became really good and was the self-proclaimed fastest gunner in our unit.

If I had stayed in that fixed mindset, I would have never become a section chief. Looking back, the ripple effect of potentially not becoming a chief would have stalled my career and my subsequent success that I've found after the military. I honestly might not even be writing this book if I had let that hold me down.

What are you letting hold you back at work? Have you hesitated to step up and volunteer to lead a meeting or a new project because you're worried you might fail? Do you hesitate to ask for feedback because you're afraid of what you might hear? Carol Dweck's research found that we can change our mindsets. Our brains are not as hardwired as we used to think. If you're letting your fear of failure hold you back, there are things that you can do. My first tip for you is that you need to understand what the expectations are. When I saw those gunners doing their jobs at a high speed, my mind automatically thought that I was expected to be like that overnight. Very rarely is that the case. Sensible people understand that it takes time, and it takes practice. First things first: understand what the expectations are of you and what your timeline is.

Managing Your Reactions

I found myself in another challenging spot when I left the Army. I had achieved the highest Army rank possible, staff sergeant, based on the amount of time in service that I had. When I left the Army, I felt like I lost my identity. And it wasn't because the rank makes you a leader; it definitely does not. It was because I had worked my way into a position where there were soldiers for whom I was directly responsible. As a college student in the civilian world, I had nothing except myself. You would think that with less responsibility, things would be easier, but it was quite the opposite for me. How could I get people to see the qualities in me if I was just another college student? It felt like I was back to the rank of private in the Army and that I was going to need to start over and work my way up.

At that time, I was attending the university where the Minnesota Vikings held their annual training camp, I was majoring in sport management, and I was very fortunate to be named the first ever NFL-Pat Tillman Military Scholar. Remember, I dropped out of a small community college in rural Minnesota when 9/11 happened. Pat Tillman gave up a multimillion-dollar contract playing for the Arizona Cardinals in the National

Football League (NFL) to become an Army Ranger, along with his brother Kevin. Unfortunately, Pat was killed in Afghanistan by friendly fire in April 2004. A few years later, his family created the Pat Tillman Foundation. I was in the second class of Tillman scholars—a very humbling cohort to be part of. Out of that cohort, the NFL and the Tillman Foundation created a new scholarship where they selected one scholar to be named the NFL-Pat Tillman Scholar. I was very honored to receive that award. It was and still is extremely humbling to even have my name associated with Pat Tillman and his acts of selflessness and service to others.

Those three things—going to school where the Vikings held training camp, majoring in sport management, and receiving the Tillman award—helped lead to my very first job outside of the Army. I was hired as a marketing intern at the Vikings training camp, and I'll never forget that first day. The person in charge of all the interns was another intern: a 21-year-old kid with a clipboard going around letting everyone know what they'd be doing for the day. He told me, "Patrick, I want to you go over there for the day." He was pointing at a big inflatable football. I was puzzled. I said, "You want me to go to the big football?" He said, "Yeah, you're going to watch the kids jump in it."

My jaw dropped. I couldn't believe what I was hearing. I had a Bronze Star Medal and a Purple Heart, three combat deployments, all that time leading soldiers on combat operations, and now I was to be relegated to watching kids jump in a bounce house? I could feel the physiological reaction my body was having. My heart raced and my hands started to shake. I felt like I was going to punch this guy in the throat! Didn't he know who I was?

Have you ever been in that situation, where something just pushes your buttons, and you must do everything you can to fight it off? Have you ever failed at fighting it off and done the throat punch? (Hopefully more metaphorically than literally.) At that time, I had a vision of working in professional sports and I knew if I let that reaction manifest into behavior, there was no way that was going to come true.

Years ago, I read a great book by Jonathan Haidt called *The Happiness Hypothesis*, which uses the analogy of the elephant and the rider. The elephant, that big, bold, majestical animal, represents our reactions, the emotional part of our brain, or the throat punch if you will. And the rider, the little tiny person on top of that strong elephant, represents our response, or our logical thinking part of our brain. Now if that little person on top has no idea what they're doing, which way do you think the elephant will go? Whichever way it wants! But just imagine if the little person on top does know what they're doing. If they have the skills, training, and experience, they can keep the elephant on the exact same path.

My second tip to help you better embrace a growth mindset is to be able to better manage your reactions. This is known as cognitive discipline, your ability to override that instinctual, conditioned, and habitual reaction and let your brain trigger a more thought-out response instead. One of the best pieces of advice that I ever received to help me do this came from a former colleague, a guy who used to fly F-16s in the Air Force. One day he asked me, "What do you think is one of the first things they taught me in fighter pilot training when an alarm would go off in the cockpit?" I told him I had no idea—probably push a bunch of buttons, call mayday on your radio, and then eject? He said the very first thing they taught him to do is to "wind the clock" back before you do anything. And they do that because you can't break anything by winding the clock. It makes your brain take that brief pause when you're going Mach 3 at 19,000 feet and an alarm goes off. It helps you override that instinctive fear-driven reaction and helps your brain trigger a more thought-out response instead. Just like we remember stop, drop, and roll, I've remembered to wind the clock.

Think about those moments in your life where you've found yourself in a fixed mindset. What were your emotions? Were you scared, nervous, maybe even fearful? Expressing emotions is great; however, if they lead us to making bad decisions or get us stuck in a fixed mindset, we need to be able to learn how to override them to make more informed and thought-out decisions.

Growing Through Who You Know

As I progressed through my academic life, I began isolating myself more and more from the outside world. I found it difficult to relate to others because they hadn't been through the same situations as I had. That certainly didn't make me see them as any less; it just made it hard for me. At the same time, I was popping pain pills to numb myself from the experiences of the previous seven years. I was headed down a very dangerous path, locked into a fixed mindset where I was letting my past failures define who I was in a very negative way—to the point where I was thinking about taking my own life.

One day in early February 2013, my phone rang. It was my friend JB Ball. I had met JB through a nonprofit organization that he founded called Tee It Up for the Troops. JB's son was deployed to Iraq and JB had asked him what he could to do support him—sending care packages and the like. His son told him to do something for those who were coming home wounded. JB created a golf event that raised money for wounded veterans. The event was such a huge success that he created this organization, which now holds golf events across the country every year and has raised over $15 million. One of the programs of this organization is putting golf clubs in the hands of wounded veterans as a means of rehabilitation—both physically and mentally. I obviously didn't grow up around a country club—in fact, I had never swung a golf club in my life until Tee It Up for the Troops put a set in my hands and turned me loose. I immediately fell in love with the game. I was and still am a terrible golfer. But I can separate the frustration of chasing a little white ball around from things that truly matter.

JB was calling because he wanted me to go with him to White Sands Missile Range in New Mexico to do the Bataan Memorial Death March. This event is held every year to honor the legacy of those who died in the Bataan Death March of World War II, when thousands of American and allied prisoners of war died while being forced by their captors to walk over 60 miles. The memorial event is 26.2 miles long—the length of a marathon. You also carry a weighted pack on your back—much like a ruck march in the military. The terrain goes from tarred roads to dirt paths to sand to concrete, along with steep elevation changes. It is not for the faint of heart. You cannot just get off the couch one day and expect to be able to do something like this. My experience in the military taught me that you need a good three to five months of training to be able to complete this kind of event. I let JB know this, several times. But he was persistent. I felt like JB could sense the road that I was going down—the isolation, the addiction—and he knew he had to do something.

Finally, after he asked me several times, I relented and agreed. But I told him there was no way I would finish. I was not prepared.

So we traveled down to New Mexico. The night before the event, there was a reception for a bunch of wounded veterans who were participating. It was my first time around a group of others who had been through similar situations. I let every single person at that reception know that I just found out about this the previous week and that there was no way I was going to be able to finish. I had to make sure that everyone knew that.

The next morning, I was near the starting line when JB introduced me to a young man. I turned around and noticed he had a prosthetic for his right leg. Nine months earlier, this young man had stepped on an IED in Afghanistan. He was participating in the event with his physical therapist from Walter Reed Hospital. I felt relieved. There was no way this guy would finish. I could just stay by him the entire time and we'd probably make it 5 or 10 miles and then give up. Boy, was I wrong. This guy broke me off at mile 14 and left me in a cloud of dust. His determination and resilience motivated me to continue to push myself and I ended up finishing the event in 6 hours and 53 minutes. My feet looked like raw hamburger by the time I was done.

It wasn't the physical nature of the accomplishment that I was most proud of. It was overcoming the obstacle that I had placed in my head—the excuses that I had let everyone know—that helped propel me into a growth mindset. That event showed me what I was capable of—that I could still do hard things. And it showed me the importance of being surrounded by like-minded people, people who are going to pick you up, and who have your best interests in mind.

Your Challenge

If you are finding yourself in a fixed mindset, don't forget to try these three tips to help develop a growth mindset:

1. Understand what is expected of you and what your timeline is. Are you starting a new job but feeling a little nervous? Ask questions and seek out opportunities to train and get better.

2. Wind the clock back. Practice cognitive discipline to help you overcome emotionally charged reactions and let you brain trigger a more thought-out response instead.

3. Surround yourself with the right people. Do you hang around someone who is always complaining or always has a negative outlook? As humans, we tend to mirror the behavior of others around us—for better or worse. It might be time to let them go and start spending time with people who are going to tell you what you need to hear, not what you want to hear.

What are some areas of your life where you might be stuck in a fixed mindset? Make a list of things that you avoid because they make you uncomfortable or that you may not be very good at it. For example, I was really stuck in a fixed mindset when it came to writing this book. For several years, people have asked me where they can get my book. I came up with a lot of excuses as to why I didn't have one. I thought it would be too hard, it would take too long, I didn't want to do it. But thanks to some great support from people who really believe in me, I have been able to shift my mindset and—ta-da!—here we are. Once you have your list, identify opportunities for you to face those challenges head on. After each opportunity, assess your growth. How have you improved?

3

Practicing Resilience

I've shared a lot about the adversity that I faced in my life. But as a society, we entered unchartered waters in early 2020 with the COVID-19 pandemic. Despite the challenges that I faced, I did not have a worldwide pandemic on my bingo card and you probably didn't either. But there we were—all of us facing a new challenge for which we were not well prepared. Every one of us was impacted, some more than others. Many people saw their jobs disappear overnight, our healthcare system was overwhelmed, education was disrupted, and who can forget about the toilet paper and supply chain shortages?!

When I reflect upon those challenges that we faced, I remember the ebbs and flows of optimism and pessimism on a near daily basis. Glimmers of hope were followed by the announcement of a new strain dragging us back down. It was tough. The mental health challenges that emerged during COVID-19 are well documented and something that many are still dealing with.

So what did we do about it? Well, we got through it. But some people managed a lot better than others. In this chapter I'm going to share my experience and some practical tips that can help you be more resilient in the face of the unknown.

Getting Bad News

In February 2019, my wife and I began the journey of adopting a child. Month after month we waited to get that call that we were matched with a birth mother. We waited so long that some of our paperwork and medical tests expired and we had to do them again. But finally, in December of 2019, we were matched with a birth mother. She was due to give birth in March of 2020.

We were over the moon excited as we shared the news with friends and family.

Anyone who has been through the adoption process will tell you that every situation is unique. We began to regularly communicate with the birth mother and paid $15,000 to help cover the agency costs and expenses for her. We even FaceTimed with her and introduced her to our two daughters, Hazelyn and Haddie. Life was good.

At the beginning of February 2020, I was pulling into the parking lot of a client in Anchorage, Alaska, to facilitate a full-day leadership workshop. My wife called me—which was a little odd because she doesn't usually reach out when she knows I'm heading to a client. I answered the phone, and I could hear the concern in her voice when she said that the adoption agency reached out and needed to speak to the both of us right away. My heart sank, I knew it was not going to be good news. I thought the birth mother had experienced a miscarriage or some other traumatic experience.

We found out that the birth mother was scamming us and the agency that we were working through. The agency had found out that she was also working through several other adoption agencies and there were other families who thought they were going to be adopting her child as well. We were devastated. The emotional investment that we made in this process far outweighed the financial loss. My wife had purchased some themed blankets, outfits, and a teddy bear for this beautiful child we were expecting. We had a name picked out. The nursery was ready. Unfortunately, we are not the only couple to have this happen to them.

I only had a few minutes to speak to my wife and gather my emotions before meeting with my client and getting set up for the workshop. It was really hard, but I knew that I was going to have to put on a brave face, not just for that day, but for my family.

One thing that helped me at that time was that I was working in an amazing job that literally took me all over the world. I got to do some great work helping organizations develop leaders at all levels in China, Africa, Europe, and all over the United States, with companies ranging from Fortune 500 organizations to small, family-owned businesses. I loved it and could not believe that I got paid money to do it. After 33 years, I felt like I had finally found what I truly wanted to do.

I had been in my role for almost five years when on February 18, 2020—while COVID-19 was still in its infancy (as far as what we knew at the time)—I got let go from that job. I had never experienced that feeling before in my life. I was down in my home office, and I cried. I was the sole income earner for our family. We were fortunate that my wife could stay home with our two daughters, but now I had no idea what we were going to do. I tried to put on a brave face as I climbed the steps from our basement to tell my wife. I didn't want her or my kids to see me crying but I couldn't hold it in. I was devastated and embarrassed. My family depended on me. Now what was I going to do?

The feelings I was experiencing were certainly not unique to me; I knew I wasn't the first person with people relying on them who ended up losing their job. I think it's safe to say that we've all received bad news in our lives—personally and professionally. It could be the unexpected loss of a loved one, a scary health diagnosis, not passing the credentialling test required for your position, being passed over for promotion, or not getting the job you applied for.

How have you reacted to those types of situations in the past? I'm going to go out on a limb here and guess that some strong emotions came into play. Did you yell at someone? Did you fire off one of those emails in ALL CAPITAL LETTERS letting them know why they made a mistake? In those situations, we can't put the toothpaste back in the tube. Fortunately, there are things that we can all do to help us be more resilient in the face of adversity.

Holding Space and Emotional Intelligence

As I sat in my office crying, my wife rubbed my back and comforted me. She is one of the best listeners I've ever met. She sat in my office with me and just held the space and allowed me to grieve. Words cannot do justice to her quiet confidence and steadfast loyalty in that moment and how I felt it throughout my body. She made me feel that everything was going to be okay.

I slowly regained my composure, and we began to discuss what the next steps should be. I figured I should start looking at job listings. But my wife wisely commented that this was my opportunity to do something different, to step outside of my comfort zone. She said, "Why don't you start your own business?"

Up until that point, I had zero desire to start my own business. Many people had mentioned it to me in the past, but I had my excuses lined up. I don't know anything about marketing. What if I messed up the taxes? I'm not good at sales. I've never done a budget. I love helping to inspire others and help them be more effective leaders, but running a business? Nah. Someone else can do that.

But as we sat and talked, she reminded me how I got to where I was: the hard work of completing a second master's degree while working full-time and having a family, the determination not to let my past define who I was, and the resilience in the face of adversity like I faced on my combat deployments. I could do difficult things. It was like I could feel the momentum shift in my head, which I now know is the dopamine release that we experience when we feel motivated and see the potential for a positive reward. I went from despair to hope. I began to seriously entertain the idea of starting a business and an hour later I was on the Secretary of State website registering a new LLC. From there, I got to work.

I slapped together a website that afternoon and made a LinkedIn post letting everyone know I was open for business. And two weeks later the world shut down due to COVID-19. Now, I would not necessarily recommend starting a new business at the beginning of a worldwide pandemic, but guess what? I am not unique. The pandemic didn't happen only to me. We've all been impacted. I viewed it as an opportunity.

When we are around someone who is experiencing adversity, many of us feel like we need to fill the air with words or platitudes to help the person going through the challenge. Although we may have the best intentions, we're not allowing them to fully process what they've experienced, and we try minimizing how they feel—usually by inserting ourselves and our own experiences in the current situation. From my experience, this does more harm than good.

On the other hand, when we allow someone to experience and express their emotions, they build their emotional intelligence. The concept of emotional intelligence (EQ) has been around for many years. We've all certainly heard of IQ and what it is. The most basic analogy that I can think of is that IQ is our book smarts while EQ is our street smarts. There is certainly more involved, but EQ is about how we understand and manage our emotions and how we recognize and influence emotions in others.

Allowing someone to express their emotions in times of adversity provides them with the opportunity to better understand and manage those emotions. When people suppress their emotions, they are also more likely to have increased levels of stress and even physical health challenges. I think it's safe to say that at one point in our lives, we've all suppressed emotions and could feel the toll it was taking on us. Some of us may have even reached a point where we let it all spill over into one huge messy outburst that probably didn't have much to do with the original problem. I've done it and it's not pretty.

In that difficult moment after losing my job, my wife held the space and allowed me to express myself. That may sound easy because she's my wife and that's what we should do for each other. But what about holding space at work—why does that matter? In a professional setting, allowing someone to express their emotions helps build higher levels of trust and can strengthen relationships. It may not always be the heaving cry I went through, but it could be a coworker expressing their frustration of being passed over for promotion or sharing their insecurities around a new project. As I've studied and experienced what high-performing teams look like, one commonality is that they have high levels of trust and have built authentic relationships with each other.

Providing space for people to express their emotions and talk about their challenges also helps them solve their own problems better. As I expressed my emotions that morning with my wife, I was able to glean some valuable clarity around what my needs and concerns really were when it came to starting my own business and overcoming all the obstacles I had in my head. This allowed me to better visualize what I needed to do to be successful. For example, I didn't need to fret about taxes. There are professionals who do that. I just need to find a good one and partner with them. That is something that seems so obvious, but when you stack up excuse after excuse, that wall of obstacles can seem daunting. Yet once you start knocking a few down, watch that wall tumble!

Surrounding Yourself with the Right People

An important lesson that I learned during my time in the military was the significance of surrounding yourself with the right people. And when I say the right people, I am talking about people who have your best interests in mind, people who are not going to tell you just what you want to hear but what you *need* to hear. In my personal life, my wife is one of those people. She has provided me unwavering emotional support as I navigated the challenges of starting my own business during a pandemic.

As I began my entrepreneurial journey, I knew I wasn't going to be able to do it all on my own and that I was going to need help. My first order of business was to reach out to my network and have conversations with people in my industry to learn about their journey and lessons learned. I also joined a professional association for our industry. I crowdsourced my knowledge through asking questions on social media. Was all the advice great? No, of course not. I would need more than two hands to count the number of people who told me that it was not a good time to start my own business.

I was quickly able to weed out the bad stuff and focus on very specific action items that I like to call "income-producing activities." Early on I learned that I did not need to sit there and spin my tires worrying about the cover image on my company's Facebook page or finding a vendor to create shirts with my logo on that. All of that could wait. I needed to make money to support my family.

Thankfully, our government had a great program in place to help businesses during the pandemic called the Paycheck Protection Program (PPP), which included forgivable loans to help businesses meet expenses and pay their employees. Whew! I felt relieved. I would have some help. Well, I quickly found out that to be eligible for a PPP loan, you needed to have started your business by February 15. I started mine on February 18. Another hurdle.

Professionally, I sought out people who could provide me with different perspectives. One thing I've noticed in my life is that we often gravitate toward those who look, think, and talk like us because we feel comfortable with them. But I was honored to work with a diverse team of soldiers in the Army and I understand the importance of diverse thought and experiences. I also searched out positive people. The pandemic brought unprecedented challenges to everyone, but I didn't have the time to be around people who spent time crying, "The sky is falling!" I wanted to be with people who filled me up, not brought me down. I found many of these attributes in other professional speakers who continue to serve as mentors to me to this day. I know that I can pick up the phone to these people and they will listen. They will give advice, but most importantly they will also hold me accountable.

I also found comfort in developing stronger social connections with those in my everyday life. In the age of social distancing, that could be tough, but I developed some great friendships with some other fathers in my neighborhood. We'd meet at the local park with our kids and just talk. It was a great break from the day-to-day grind of trying to start a business. This might be a little surprising to hear from someone who speaks for a living, but I am very much an introvert at heart. But I cannot express enough the importance of being part of a community and the sense of belonging and how it impacts our emotional resolve when dealing with adversity. I had to force myself outside of my comfort zone, but I am glad I did.

What can you do to surround yourself with the right people? It's never a bad idea to evaluate who is in your circle and who you are letting influence you. Are there people around you who just seem to be negative all the time or are always complaining? It might be time to give them a little space or, better yet, you can be the person who lifts them up by helping them overcome the negativity that's impacting their life. It's not an easy role but it's very rewarding and can help you be more resilient as well.

I encourage you to find mentors to help you grow. And don't just blindly do what your people advise. Weigh their advice and determine what will really work best for you. If you don't have these types of people in your life right now, go find them. You need to be proactive. From a professional standpoint, LinkedIn is a great tool to use to find others who could be valuable sounding boards for you. They might work in your industry or even at the same company. Try to find common connection points; maybe you both started out in the same position or attended the same school, or you grew up where they live now. And be authentic when you reach out to this person.

Maintaining Perspective

I was working hard to start my business during a global pandemic, but hiring a motivational leadership speaker was not at the top of everyone's list. (I could certainly argue about why it *should* be important, but I digress.) As my wife and I faced the reality of the financial challenges that lay before us, I knew we had to make some changes. My previous job provided me with a salary that allowed us to live very comfortably. Changes were now needed. We had a little bit of money in our savings but that had been earmarked for the adoption. And a good chunk of that was lost during the failed match that we experienced. We had to go against all conventional wisdom and sound financial advice and tap into our 401(k) just to make ends meet.

As the days slowly dragged on and after a lot of prayerful consideration, my wife and I decided to continue on the adoption journey. We could have easily given up; I don't think anyone would have thought less of us if we did. In late May of 2020, my wife was visiting her parents back home with our two daughters. They lived about two and a half hours from us in a small town in southwestern Minnesota. I stayed home to continue to work on my business. When we decided to continue the adoption process, we began to receive emails letting us know of potential birth mothers. We would then need to decide if we wanted to have our portfolio presented to the birth mother. This portfolio is a book that includes pictures and information on our family. In the adoption world, birth mothers are usually presented with many portfolios from which they must select a family.

It was a Tuesday afternoon when we received one of those emails asking us if we would like to present our portfolio to a birth mother. This situation was a little unique compared to others that we had seen because the birth mother had actually just given birth on Sunday to a healthy baby girl. I called my wife right away to see if she had seen the email. We both agreed that we wanted to present the portfolio. We'd been in this situation many times, and many times we got our hopes up, only to be let down when we were not chosen. I couldn't put my finger on it, but something felt different with this one. A few hours later we received a call from the adoption agency saying that the birth mother was really interested in us and was requesting some more information. We knew that we had a chance, but I was trying my best to temper my expectations. Again, we'd been down this road before.

My wife was unsure what to do. Should she start driving the two and a half hours back home in case we got picked and needed to fly out in the morning? She could just leave our daughters with her parents. We got that answer just before midnight when we were told that the birth mother had chosen us, and we needed to get down to Houston as soon as possible. My wife quickly packed up, kissed our girls goodbye, and made the drive home. I immediately booked our flight and packed my bag. We had no idea how long we would be gone because state law required us to physically remain in the adoption state until paperwork could be processed, which could take anywhere from 3 to 21 business days. My wife arrived very late that night (actually early morning) and we snatched a few hours of sleep before we headed to the airport, although I don't think either of us really slept much with the excitement and nervous tension running through our bodies.

We grabbed a quick bite to eat at the airport before our plane took off. We could not believe we were finally doing this. We landed in Houston, got our rental car, and headed for the hospital. It was pouring rain. Prior to going into the hospital, we sat in the car and said a prayer for the birth mother. Despite all of our excitement for this day, we knew that it would not be easy for her. We could not imagine the feelings she was experiencing at that moment.

Once inside the hospital, we were taken to a small room with a social worker where we started to fill out an endless stack of paperwork. As we were finishing up, the door opened, and a nurse pushed in a small cart with a beautiful baby girl swaddled in a blanket. Behind her was the birth mother, tears in her eyes and tissues in her hand. We both stood up and went to give her a hug. This woman was making a very courageous decision, and we were humbled and honored that she had chosen us.

Inside that nondescript hospital room, we met our beautiful daughter Haven for the first time. We took turns holding her as her birth mother shared more about her life and her family. She worked full-time and was a single mother to three kids between the ages of 8 and 14. She had her hands full, and she knew it. She wanted the best for her daughter. After a few hours, we said our goodbyes. It was really hard to watch her hold Haven one last time. As we walked out of the hospital with Haven in her car seat carrier, we could not believe that just 24 hours prior, we were sitting in Minnesota with zero idea this was about to happen. We spent less than a week at a hotel in Houston and were finally able to come home. It was amazing to introduce our two daughters to their new sister.

I mentioned earlier the ebbs and flows of emotions we all experienced during the pandemic. The gravity of the situation definitely exacerbated those feelings, but at the same time we've all been on that roller coaster of emotions at different points in our lives. The adoption journey we navigated was full of highs and lows. But we often reminded each other that we needed to let go of things that were out of our control. That is a lot easier said than done, especially for someone like me who likes to have control, or at least know what tomorrow will bring.

I vividly remember the ups and downs during my time in the military, specifically as it related to changing missions during our combat deployments. It would usually look like this: someone would say they heard from someone else that we were moving to a new location and that location was getting attacked every day and it was the worst place to be, then someone else would add to that they heard about that place too and they knew someone who was there before and how bad it was. And that rumor would continue until the official announcement from our command on our change of mission, or it wouldn't even happen at all. I learned early on the importance of accepting that there were things that I could not control. One of the things that helped me better be able to do this was just to make a simple list. Control on one side and not control on the other with a line down the middle of the page. For me, it helped to visualize these things that better helped me accept what I could not control and, just as importantly, gain more clarity around what I could control.

What does that look like for you? Are there rumors going around that your company is going to be acquired by a competitor? Are people talking about potential layoffs or budget cutbacks? Whatever the situation is, the sooner you are able to accept that there are things out of your control, the sooner you are able to put more effort and focus in those in which you can. I can't control whether my company is going to be bought out, but I can continue to work hard and show my value to this company. Or I could dust off and update my resume, in case I need it. Both of those are much more productive than ruminating on the unknown that is out of your control.

As new problems arise, I've also learned over time the value of reflecting on past situations in helping me to keep things in perspective. We've all faced adversity before and we're going to face it again. When a new challenge arises, I take time to reflect on how I navigated past situations that are similar. What worked well for me? What wouldn't I do again? What resources do I have to help me?

Your Challenge

Make a list of five people who have had a positive impact on you in your life. Write down what each of them did and how they helped you. Try to be as specific as possible. Send them a short message (text or email) to tell them what they did for you and how it impacted you. Want a bigger challenge? Call them and tell them!

Now, make a list of three people in your professional circle whom you care about and want to see succeed. Reach out to these people and have a conversation around what their goals are and ask how you can help them achieve those goals. Having a mentor is great and has helped me overcome a lot of challenges, but being a mentor is extremely rewarding and will also help you continue to be more resilient in the face of adversity.

4

Continuous Improvement

In early 2005 our unit was preparing to deploy to Afghanistan. I knew that I was going to have a big decision to make while on this deployment because my initial enlistment contract with the Army was nearing its end. I could choose to get out of the Army after this deployment and pursue a new challenge in the civilian world or I could reenlist and stay in the Army for a few more years. I knew that I needed to focus on the upcoming deployment, but I would be lying if I said this decision did not weigh heavily on my mind. If I chose to reenlist, there were a few different options that were available to me, including changing jobs, applying for flight school, or even trying out for the Army Special Forces.

I was 22 years old at this time and a newly promoted sergeant. I had been promoted ahead of all of my peers, and my responsibilities during this deployment would be different than when I was a lower enlisted soldier in Iraq. In the section "Committing to Your Path" in Chapter 1, I mentioned some advice that served me well early on in my military career: "Do what you're told, do what you're told, do what you're damn well told." I was proud of what I had accomplished thus far but I knew that mantra would not take me to where I wanted to be. Honestly, I was not quite sure exactly what that was, but a desire was stirring inside of me that told me I could not just rest on my laurels. Whether I was going to stay in the Army or get out, I needed to continue to take advantage of every opportunity in front of me to better myself, both personally and professionally.

Why should this matter for you? Look at how technology has evolved and the expansion of global markets. Even if you're new to your position, think back 5 or 10 years ago on how they were doing things. I would imagine that things have changed. By continuing your development, you are increasing your capability to be adaptable and up-to-date in an ever-changing industry and world.

In this chapter, I am going to share some of the steps I have taken to continue my development. We're all on a unique path in life, but the fact that you are here right now, reading Chapter 4, tells me one thing about you: you are not satisfied with where your development is at. You know that there is more out there for you to achieve. You want to grow and develop and get better at things. The specific things that I did to better myself may not work for you. But the point is for you to be proactive and find those things that connect to your purpose and goals and pursue them.

Learning While Working

We deployed to Afghanistan on March 3, 2005, exactly one year to the date of when we returned from Iraq. Our artillery battery consisted of four platoons, with two howitzer sections in every platoon. Each platoon was assigned to a different forward operating base (FOB) in Regional Command East in Afghanistan. Basically, our unit was going to be spread throughout remote FOBs near the Pakistani border. We were all tasked with providing indirect fire support for ground troops. My platoon was tasked to work specifically with special operations forces, including US Army Special Forces, Navy SEALs, and other government agencies.

As a traditional Army unit, we had done very little work with special operations forces, outside of some early artillery raids during the initial push into Iraq in 2003. This deployment, we worked and lived directly with these units. There was definitely a culture clash. Special operations forces in the military have a more laid-back culture when it comes to their attire and appearance. As an airborne unit, we prided ourselves on maintaining the highest standards all the time. I will never forget when we first arrived at the FOB that we would call home for the next 12 months. There was a little shock at first when we saw these bearded men coming out to the landing zone; some were in flipflops and backwards ball caps, others in cut-off-sleeve shirts, and way outside the normal regulation hair. It took a little while, but we eventually developed a great relationship with these special operation units, and we saved their butts a few times with our artillery fire as well. This is a valuable lesson that people coming from different work cultures with different approaches and priorities can respect each other and work very effectively together toward shared goals.

One of the things I remember most about this location was how dark it would get. If the moon was not up, you literally could not see your hand in front of your face at night. There was no ambient light of cities shining off the sky in the distance. It was nothing but darkness and a never-ending ceiling of stars as far as the eye could see. It was beautiful but it definitely served as a reminder that we were in one of the most remote locations in the world. I live in a rural area right now and when I see the glow of small-town lights in the distance, I am reminded of the experiences I had during my time in Afghanistan.

Despite being in one of the most remote locations in the world, we had a pretty decent internet connection thanks to the special operations forces we worked with. They had bigger budgets and had all the cool toys and technology. I was living in a literal mud hut near the Pakistani border, but I had a good connection to the outside world. With the help and encouragement of my platoon leader, Jon Post, I enrolled in a program called EArmyU. This program allowed soldiers to take online college courses through schools back in the United States. The Army would cover 100% of the tuition and books and it would not dip into our GI Bill benefits. My goal was to finish all of my general study courses, two years' worth of traditional college, so that if and when I left the Army, I could go straight into my choice of major.

I enrolled in this program in late summer of 2005 and soon started taking online classes through a small school called Central Texas College, which does a lot of work with active military members. The faculty were very understanding of our current challenges, and I appreciated the fact that these courses were all work-at-your-own-pace-type classes. We obviously did not have a very predictable schedule with our missions, so this allowed me the chance to knock down big chunks of the coursework in one sitting.

The ability to work at my own pace in my classes was great but I still had to take traditional midterms and finals, albeit over the computer. I remember one instance when I was in the middle of a final exam for my American government class when we were attacked with indirect fire. I was in our Tactical Operations Center (TOC) working on the computer when I heard the first explosion hit. I rushed out of the TOC and ran down to our gun, and we started returning fire. By the time everything had quieted down, I returned to the TOC to find out that my test had timed out. I ended up receiving a D on the test. I would imagine many professors have heard some very creative excuses from students on why they didn't complete their assignment—the proverbial dog ate my homework—but I would bet that coming under attack by rockets was not one of them. Thankfully, my professor, a Vietnam veteran, was very understanding and allowed me the opportunity to take my test again.

I still was not sure if I was going to stay in the Army. But working with the Special Forces soldiers allowed me the unique perspective to see how they operate and provided an opportunity to ask them a lot of questions about their work as trying out for them had been one potential route I was exploring. I really enjoyed working with these soldiers—the best of the best, well trained, well equipped, and very smart. One of the Special Forces team members that I grew close with told me that most Special Forces soldiers (though certainly not all) end up making a career out of the military. The thought of making that type of decision scared me. I wasn't ready to commit that much of my life to the military at that time. So I made the decision that Special Forces was not the route I wanted to take.

In December of 2005 I decided to reenlist in the Army for three more years. I still was not sure what I wanted to do but I knew that I really enjoyed the people I was with and the unit I was in, so I figured it wouldn't hurt to keep doing that until I became clearer on what I wanted out of my future. I ended up finishing all of my general study courses, two years' worth of traditional college, between both of my deployments to Afghanistan.

Seeking Out New Opportunities

It's not uncommon for people to work for several different companies (or even in different fields) in their professional career. The idea of climbing the corporate ladder has been replaced with navigating a jungle gym. Sometimes you're moving left or right, or maybe even a small step back, to get to where you ultimately want to go. Continuing your development is a great opportunity for you to differentiate yourself if you're vying for a coveted promotion or if you're competing against others for a new job. In Chapter 2 we talked about embracing a growth mindset and understanding the importance of stepping outside of our comfort zone to try something different. Those opportunities are not always going to be the phone ringing with a friend like JB inviting you to do a grueling physical challenge that you were not prepared for. More often than not, you're going to have to get out there and find those opportunities yourself.

Continuing to improve doesn't always mean you're working full time and going back to college. An abundance of resources is available to help you in your journey, and many of them are free. LinkedIn Learning is a great resource, as are many of the numerous free leadership training courses from top universities in the United States. Try to find the opportunities that are relevant to your field and can help boost your credentials. I am fortunate to speak at a lot of conferences and there are always great education sessions available to participants. Do you want to really step outside of your comfort zone? I challenge you to actually submit a speaker proposal to your industry's leading conference to facilitate your own breakout session on a topic you are passionate about.

One of the most overlooked opportunities to continue your development is within your own company's internal training programs. Many clients I have partnered with have a robust online learning management system with almost every topic you could imagine. The biggest problem I've found is that many employees have no idea that it even exists. Please take advantage of these opportunities that your employer provides for you.

A lot of professional associations will also host regular webinars related to industry-leading topics. I know everyone is busy and all of this certainly sounds good and is a lot easier said than done. I never said it would be easy, but take a second to look at those who are high achievers. One thing they have in common is they've worked hard to earn what they have. It might take you being very intentional with your time and specifically carving out an hour or two each week in your calendar to spend time on your organization's learning management system or to go back and watch an industry-specific webinar.

Transitioning Development Is an Ongoing Journey

As I mentioned in Chapter 1, I had to navigate some obstacles to get accepted into college after the Army. I did that while I was still in Afghanistan on my last deployment. Another thing I did to help set me up for success was to apply for scholarships. One in particular had caught my attention, the Horatio Alger Military Scholarship. Horatio Alger was a well-known author of many books in which characters overcame the adversity of their past to be very successful. This obviously really resonated with me. I submitted my application along with a personal essay and was very humbled when I received the news that I was selected.

Since I had finished all of my general studies, I was able to double-major in history and sport management. I joked earlier in the book how I felt like the old man on campus and that was partially true. Many of my friends from high school were getting married, starting families, and had a firm hold on their professional careers. I knew I had to put the pedal down, so I even took classes over the summer because I felt like I was playing catchup with my peers. In hindsight, I realize I didn't need to do that because I've discovered we all have our own unique journey and we set ourselves up for failure and letdown when we compare ourselves to others. I had to chart my own path.

I had applied for an internship with the local independent baseball team in the town where I was going to college. This was prior to my time interning with the Minnesota Vikings. I was so excited for this opportunity, and I was so confident I would get the job. The person who interviewed me was a couple of years younger than I was and had just graduated college two years prior. I felt like I aced that interview. But a few weeks later, I was informed that I did not receive the position. A year later, I spoke at an event for our school and the general manager (GM) of that baseball team was in attendance. The GM came up to me afterwards and offered me an internship on the spot. I politely declined.

I finished my bachelor's degree and still had a couple of years remaining on my GI Bill benefits thanks to taking the online college courses through EArmyU. I immediately began graduate school and managed to complete my master's degree in sport management in one year by taking extra classes each semester and again over the summer. I felt for sure that my days of writing papers and taking tests were now behind me. Boy, was I wrong!

I had been working with a small leadership development firm for a little over a year when they offered me the opportunity to continue my professional development by seeking out a certification-type program. I was leading a lot of leadership development workshops for a variety of clients, so I sought out a program that aligned with what I was doing and that could help me level up. I found such a program at Georgetown University in the Executive Certificate in Facilitation. This was a cohort-based program that met for several days once a month over a three-month period, with coursework in between. This also provided me a great opportunity to network with others who were doing similar work to me. It definitely helped me become a better facilitator and it helped that I had a very supportive employer.

The next year, I was challenged to go deeper with my development. I was asked to find a master's program relevant to my work. This was going to be a much bigger commitment than the short certification program I did through Georgetown. My wife had just given birth to our second daughter, and I was traveling quite a bit for work. How in the world was I going to go back to school full-time and juggle everything else? Thankfully, many programs are available that cater exactly toward people in my position and I found a great one at Pepperdine University.

The Master of Science in Organization Development (MSOD) program at Pepperdine is hailed as one of the best in the country. The faculty are very experienced professionals in the organization development (OD) field, with many of them learning directly under the pioneers of the industry such as Schein, Chris Argyris, and Warren Bennis, to name a few. The program really attracted me, with its balance of theoretical and practical application, along with its global perspective. My employer at the time was again very supportive of my professional development journey, and I still had a little bit of my GI Bill benefits left that could help cover some of the expenses.

At the time, this program was designed to meet six times in person over two years. We met three times in the United States and three times in international locations: France, Costa Rica, and China. We got to do a lot of hands-on work with real-world clients, and the connection we built as a cohort was extremely strong. Many of us stay in touch to this day and reach out to each other for advice. The capstone of the program was a traditional thesis, and I was not especially excited about this. I mentioned in Chapter 2 that I am not big on writing, and that thesis was the most challenging thing I have done from an academic perspective. But I would not change a thing. It made me step outside of my comfort zone and do something that was going to take a lot of effort. I successfully completed this program in 2019 and I am forever grateful for the people I met on that journey.

Being SMART About Setting Goals

To this day, I continue to seek out opportunities to better myself personally and professionally. I am working toward very specific goals, and I seek out those opportunities I feel are going to help me achieve those goals. When it comes to goal setting, I use the popular SMART framework to help develop mine.

Whether setting goals in your personal or your professional life, the SMART acronym can be tremendously helpful. SMART stands for Specific, Measurable, Achievable, Relevant, and Time-bound:

- **Specific:** Clearly define the goal. Be as precise as you can about what you want to accomplish.
- **Measurable:** Establish specific criteria for measuring progress toward achieving your goal.

- **Achievable:** It is very important that the goal is realistic and attainable. It should be challenging enough to motivate you, but not so difficult that it becomes demoralizing. Take into consideration your available resources and even the constraints you face.

- **Relevant:** The goal should be relevant to your life, personally or professionally, and it should align with your values.

- **Time-bound:** Set a specific time frame for achieving the goal. Having a specific deadline also provides a time frame for evaluating your progress.

Here is an example of a goal that I am currently working toward:

I want to be part of the Million-Dollar Speakers Club by the end of 2026. I track my progress toward this goal monthly and the work that I do is focused on helping me achieve that goal.

- Specific: The Million Dollar Club is a prestigious group in the National Speakers Association of professional speakers who bring in $1,000,000 in revenue from their speaking business in one year.

- Measurable: $1,000,000 in revenue is easy to track with online accounting software.

- Achievable: It's definitely a stretch goal but something that is actually achievable with hard work.

- Relevant: I am a professional speaker; it's what I do.

- Time-bound: I have until the end of 2026 and I monitor this information monthly.

Your Challenge

How have you continued to develop yourself? It doesn't always involve going back to school; heck, it could mean reading this book. It's a great start. Are you part of a professional association? Does your career require continuing education units?

Create or refine a goal that you have for yourself that you want to accomplish in the next one to three years. Use the SMART acronym to help you. Be sure to break down the Specific, Measurable, Achievable, Relevant, and Time-bound aspects on separate lines, as I did for my Million-Dollar Speakers Club goal in the "Being SMART About Setting Goals" section earlier in this chapter.

Leading Teams

The first part of this book focused on leading yourself. From discovering your purpose to cultivating a growth mindset, you've explored ideas and techniques to help you better lead yourself. In Part II, the focus shifts to how you can more effectively lead teams while continuing to employ practical tips and challenges that you can start implementing. Let's dive in.

5

Leading by Example

f you want to build and effectively lead a high-performing team, there need to be high levels of trust. Although we all pretty much know that, I've found that it's one thing to know what good leadership looks like but it's a completely different thing to actually put into action. We often think of leadership as a sublime experience akin to leading soldiers up the proverbial hill in battle with bullets whizzing by, but in all actuality it's the consistent application of the small things, such as being empathetic, being a good listener, meeting the needs of others, maintaining commitments, and so on, that establishes our leadership credibility. Please don't get me wrong; I've served with and met some of the most courageous people in the world who actually charged up hills with bullets whizzing by, but most of them will tell you it does not take a grandiose gesture like that to be a good leader.

The number one way to start building trust with others is to lead by example. When we lead by example, this creates alignment between our words and our actions and it demonstrates to others exactly what our expectations are. Imagine you lead a small team and you have a weekly team meeting but every week, like clockwork, you're 10 minutes late. Yet when one of your colleagues is running late to meet with you or misses a deadline, you get upset. You might be thinking to yourself, it's just 10 minutes to a lousy team meeting, but what kind of message does that send? Remember, it's the consistent application of the small things that makes a leader credible and effective.

In this chapter, I am going to share with you the worst mistake of my life while also providing practical tips to help you better lead by example. I don't think I would be writing this book or traveling the world inspiring others and influencing the future if it were not for this event. I am very used to telling this story live and in-person—it's an emotional experience that impacts a lot of listeners. I hope that my words in these next few pages will do justice to the people who were involved in the events that took place.

Incoming!

On June 8, 2005, I was operating with our platoon out of a small forward operating base (FOB) near the Pakistani border with Afghanistan at place called FOB Shkin. Etched into one of the walls of the Alamo—a fortress of hardened mud that served as the main operations area of the FOB—was something that I will never forget. It said, "You are now at the tip of the spear and the end of the line. When you're short on everything, except the enemy, you're at FOB Shkin." This was the location we just talked about in the last chapter, where we worked exclusively with the Army Special Forces, Navy SEALs, and other governmental agencies by providing indirect fire support from our howitzer cannons.

On this particular morning, we were expecting two different helicopter flights, with the first being some Blackhawk helicopters carrying our outgoing commander, Major J. Shay Howard, and our incoming commander, Major Ryker Horn. They were coming to conduct their change of command ceremony and to spend some time with their troops. The other flight we were expecting was a couple of Chinook helicopters that were going to be bringing us a resupply of our artillery ammunition.

Any time we would have helicopters come in, one gun team was designated as the hot gun, which meant they would stay ready and man the howitzer in case we got attacked, while the other gun team was responsible for unloading whatever supplies were onboard the helicopter. On this day, my team was the designated hot gun. But the other team had a sergeant who was getting on that helicopter to go on a two-week R&R. Prior to the helicopters coming in, our platoon leadership tasked me with backfilling that sergeant's position while he was gone. I was excited for this because my buddies Luke and Landon were in that team and I would get to spend some more time with them.

As soon as we heard the distant "thump-thump" of the Chinook's double rotor blades cresting the mountains, I hopped in the front passenger seat of a Humvee and Luke hopped in the driver's seat. As we were about to pull away to drive to the landing zone, my soldier, Emmanuel Hernandez, hopped in the back. He was supposed to stay back with the hot gun, so I turned around and was about to yell at him. But I thought for a second about how I valued this kind of work ethic. He was volunteering to come lift some heavy boxes and help the team out. Awesome! I knew that our team, the hot gun, would be okay without him. So I didn't say anything.

As I was turning back around, out of the corner of my eye, I noticed he didn't have his helmet on. I literally opened my mouth and was about to yell at him, but then I realized that I didn't have mine on either. It's kind of hard for me to say something to someone else if I myself am not doing the right thing. So I said nothing.

As the helicopter landed, a group of 10 of us had to step to the side of the aircraft so they could get the machine gun off the back ramp, and we could start unloading it. We couldn't hear each other as the rotor blades were turning but my platoon sergeant handed me a piece of paper with serial numbers on it for some other items we were expecting—basically telling me it was my responsibility to make sure we got those specific items.

I grabbed the piece of paper and turned my back to the group so I could guide my buddy Luke in the Humvee to get him a little closer to the back of the helicopter. The next thing I knew, *boom!* and everything went dark. It was as if I was hit on the back of the head and just crumbled to the ground. As I was lying there, disoriented and unable to hear, my first thought was maybe someone was playing a joke—just soldiers horsing around—or maybe one of the big engines on the back of the helicopter had a malfunction. But then my nose caught a whiff of a strong, acrid smell that hung in the air and stung my nostrils. My head felt like it had been put in a blender set on high, but after a few seconds I opened my eyes and sat up and saw there were bodies and blood all over the ground.

My hearing slowly came back, and I heard the whirring sound of the helicopter as it powered down. There was a moment of eerie silence that felt like it lasted two seconds and two hours at the same time. But that silence was pierced by a whistling sound I was all too familiar with, an incoming rocket. I quickly got up and dove underneath the Humvee for cover as rockets started to impact all around. I was digging my fingernails tight into the rock-covered ground hugging the earth, hoping a rocket would not hit the helicopter that was loaded with pallets of 105mm artillery ammunition. I quickly realized it was a rocket that had landed next to us that had knocked me down. As the barrage finally ended, I crawled out from under the Humvee and started making my way back to the soldiers who were still on the ground, unsure of what I was going to find.

I had almost made it to the first soldier when a Marine who was training the Afghan National Army on our base yelled to me that I had been hit. I hadn't felt any pain at that point, but I turned my head and saw that the back of my uniform was shredded, with patches of blood soaking through. It was at that moment that the pain all of a sudden hit me.

The other soldiers quickly triaged those of us who were wounded and loaded us into whatever type of vehicle they could find and brought us to the small clinic on our base that was run by an Afghan doctor who treated the locals. My wounds were very minor compared to everyone else's. I was peppered in the back with small pieces of shrapnel—a few small holes, nothing too serious—but it definitely hurt!

In the Army, this is what we call a mass casualty situation. As the other soldiers treated the more severely wounded, I wandered around in a state of shock trying to help. Luke came up to me and began to bandage me up. He patched up the small holes in my back along with a large cut that sliced me open on the right side of my torso. A Special Forces soldier who was walking by pulled out his multitool, opened the pliers, and pulled out a small piece of shrapnel that was still sticking out of my lower back. I was in disbelief that he did that but also disappointed that he just threw the piece to the side because I wanted to get a look at it.

Luke finished placing my left arm in a sling because any movement of it caused an immense amount of pain, and that is when I saw Sergeant Michael Kelly, a supply sergeant from Scituate, Massachusetts, who was recently attached to our unit, lying on an elevated stretcher and the local Afghan doctor—a real short guy—standing on a red milk create performing CPR.

I did a quick lap around the clinic to see who else was hurt and I came across my platoon sergeant, Damon Burnett, the one who had handed me the piece of paper right before the explosion. He was lying on a stretcher outside the clinic, which was already full with others who were hurt. He had a tourniquet on his left leg because his femoral artery was severed, along with other severe wounds to his wrist and abdomen. And it couldn't have been more than 45 seconds when I came back around and saw they had lowered Michael to the ground and were zipping him up into a body bag.

I eventually found my way to a small room in the back of the clinic, and that's where I found my soldier, Emmanuel Hernandez, being worked on as he lay on a rudimentary hospital-type bed. His head was bandaged, and he was unconscious—but I could see his chest rise and fall so I knew he was breathing. I grabbed his hand and whispered to him that everything was going to be okay.

Several different medevac helicopters arrived shortly after and flew the wounded to forward surgical teams spread throughout Afghanistan. Another wounded soldier on this flight was from the radar team attached to our unit. He had taken a piece of shrapnel through his bicep and was in a state of shock. I remember him throwing up while on the flight. Also on the helicopter was Damon Burnett, who by that point was unconscious due to the amount of blood that he'd lost. Things were not looking too good for him, but thanks to the quick thinking of our soldiers on the ground who put the tourniquet on his leg and the surgical team, he survived, and he kept his leg.

The surgical team removed several small pieces of shrapnel from my back but left a few souvenirs in there that were too deep to get out. They stitched and patched me up and I was sent out to the landing zone to get on another helicopter to Bagram Airfield for more advanced medical care. As I was waiting there, my commander, Major Howard, approached me and asked how I was doing. I told him I was going to be okay, and I asked him about Emmanuel. He told me that he was going to be okay, and I felt so relieved.

He turned to walk away but didn't get more than four or five steps when he turned around, and with tears coming down his cheeks, he said, "I am sorry. I lied. Hernandez didn't make it." My knees got weak, and I hit the ground as Major Howard embraced me. Emmanuel died because shrapnel from the explosion hit him in the head. He died because I wasn't leading by example. Because I didn't have the courage to do the right thing or to speak up. And of course, there have been so many days since then where I have thought how simple it would have been if I had just said, "Hey guys, wait a second, let's go grab our helmets." It would have taken a matter of moments. Nothing would have been delayed.

Just that morning at breakfast, Emmanuel had been telling another soldier how he couldn't wait to get home and start having kids. And if only I had done the right thing, his wife, Jessica, would still have her husband; his mother, Ellie, would still have her son; and he would have his life ahead of him.

Setting the Example

This chapter began with a discussion about the importance of trust. As I described in the previous section, I broke that trust with my soldiers on June 8, 2005, by not leading by example. We had an understood trust in each other to have each other's back, whether that meant trusting the person responsible for being awake in the middle of the night on guard duty or trusting that we speak up when we noticed someone was not doing the right thing, like wearing their helmet. For a long time after that incident, I went down a dark path and beat myself up pretty badly. I obviously cannot change the past, but I have learned that I can take that story and influence the future.

If you're not actively deployed in the military somewhere around the world, I can say, with a strong amount of certainty, that you probably will not get rockets shot at you. Obviously, not every decision will have life-or-death consequences, and thank goodness for that! But the idea of you being able to inspire and influence those around you through the consistent application of good leadership behaviors cannot be overstated. It might be as simple as you choosing to share information with a colleague that will save them some growing pains during the project they are working on. Or it could be as simple as picking up a water bottle, which leads us to a story that really encapsulates the importance of leading by example.

My friend Jeff is a high-performing manager for a client of mine. He and I partnered together to do some really great work with the front-line employees of the Fortune 500 organization Jeff works for. He has risen through the ranks of the organization ahead of his peers because he cares about people, he is proactive, and he is innovative. He was promoted to a position where he oversaw several different projects. Like a good leader, Jeff made it a priority to get out to every project and to get to know his team. At these sites, the project manager would take him on a tour of their project. The eyes of the crews were undoubtedly monitoring their every move as they wondered, who is this guy? Why is he here?

One of the questions Jeff would ask was "What's one of your biggest challenges when it comes to people?" During one such visit, without missing a beat, the project manager said, "I can't get these idiots to keep this place clean. See what I mean?" And right after he said that he kicked a dusty water bottle that was blowing in the wind on the site. Just as that happened, Jeff looked up and saw the eyes of the entire crew peering down on them from an elevated platform. They had heard every word and seen the project manager kick the lonely water bottle.

When you're faced with a situation like the one with that project manager, it's easy to get frustrated. But it's also an opportunity. You can lead by example by trying to show him to lead by example. Regardless of whether your attempts with that specific project manager work, others will see it or hear about it, and you'll be leading them by example, too. Here are just a few of the options you could try:

1. You could explain to the project manager that calling his crew idiots doesn't encourage them to respect his guidance and follow his instructions.
2. You could explain to the project manager that he should pick up the bottle himself, and not make a big negative-energy display of doing so.
3. You could do the above two items away from the team's eyes, so the project manager doesn't need to get defensive and might be more receptive to changing his approach.

4. You could start looking into the other teams and project managers to determine if this is part of a wider pattern of workplace culture that could be addressed across teams.

5. You could consider whether the teams could use further training about keeping the worksites clean.

6. You could consider whether the project managers could use further training about how to lead their people.

7. You could also consider the culture of the teams and how the language you choose to use in addressing them might be more effective. (In some workplace environments, if you communicate the wrong way, the entire team rolls their eyes. But if you know how to speak in the way they want to be reached, you can sometimes get great results.)

8. In all of the above instances of communication and training, you can make sure that you're modeling the same behavior you want from the teams and project managers. Treat them with dignity and respect, and exhibit the same behaviors you're asking them to do.

9. It doesn't always have to be a big production. For example, if you're dealing with messy worksites, you could start or end the work shift by having the whole team take 10 minutes to clean up the place, and the project manager can participate in this with the team—in a positive, pleasant way.

Whether you're a project manager, team leader, mid-level manager, or outside contractor, you can try to implement these and other actions, and while doing so model the proper behavior for your people. That's leading by example.

Were all of these ideas implemented in the scenario Jeff dealt with? No. Sometimes there are time and money considerations, organizational focuses, competing priorities, or other constraints that affect what you can do. And sometimes you have so many responsibilities to manage that you don't think of every potential option at the moment. And that's okay, too. Acknowledging the reality that you're human and that you have parameters within which you have to work is also leading by example.

Put yourself in the shoes of one of those crew members. You hear the project manager, your boss, refer to your crew as idiots and then you see him kick a bottle instead of picking it up—something he has complained about for the last couple of weeks. How would you feel? Through his choice of words and his action of kicking the water bottle, that project manager lost all credibility—the little bit he probably had with the crew, and all that he had with Jeff. Trust me, it's the small things that we need to get right on a consistent basis to lead others effectively.

Putting It into Practice

As humans, we tend to mirror the behavior of others around us. If I'm not wearing my helmet on that landing zone in Afghanistan, how can I expect Emmanuel to do the same? The good news is it works for the good stuff as well! Here are five things that you can do to better lead by example—regardless of what your job is, what industry you work in, or what title you have (especially because having a title is not what makes you a leader).

1. **Seek work-life balance:** We've heard so much about the importance of work-life balance and self-care over the last several years that some of us cringe when we hear it. And we do that because it's one thing to say we value it but it's another thing to actually live it. Emails sent late at night can

set a bad precedent. I understand that this is when some people get the most work done—we all have different schedules and commitments in our personal lives. But think of the precedent that might set for others. I sometimes write emails late at night, but there is a great feature now where you can schedule when you want to send it. I may write it in the evening, but I will schedule it to be sent out in the morning.

2. **Practice punctuality:** Please be on time. I know things come up, other meetings go long, an unexpected phone call comes in, and the like. Do your best to communicate those if they happen. But if you are consistently late, it leaves the impression that you don't value other people's time. The ability to be on time is also a reflection of our self-discipline and our ability to manage and prioritize our commitments.

3. **Be approachable:** During my time in the Army and my work in the civilian sector, I've worked with some pretty tough-looking people. They would be the first to tell you they are not very approachable. But think about how that might impact others. Maybe you have a new employee who has an important question to ask but they see a scowl on your face. I guarantee you they feel apprehensive about coming to you with a question. I'm not saying you need to be all sunshine and unicorns all day with a permanent smile, but you're smart and you know what I am saying. Your attitude can be contagious and impact team morale.

4. **Stay engaged:** Actively participate in team projects and collaborations. We can tell when others mentally check out. It might be in that weekly project update meeting. If you hop straight on your phone or computer after giving your update and don't pay attention to others, it sets a bad example, and you are missing a valuable opportunity to contribute to the team's success. On the opposite side, it's important to strike a

balance and not dominate the conversation and to actively encourage others to participate and share their opinions.

5. **Strive for continuous improvement:** We talked in Chapter 4 about the importance of this but think about it from the perspective of leading by example. If others see you investing in your own development, what do you think it could do for them? I love facilitating leadership development workshops. Often, clients will allow anyone in the organization to attend—which I think is great. But it never fails that people sometimes say something to the effect of "Why isn't my boss in here? They really need to hear this." If you have people for whom you are directly responsible, you should not only be encouraging them to continue their development but should also be taking advantage of it yourself. When I think of the hundreds of organizations that I have been honored to work with, the most admired leaders are the ones who intentionally take time out of their day for their own development and spend time with their people.

Your Challenge

Write a list of the top five things you value in a leader. Now think about the past seven days, and write down the ways that you have lived those values. Be specific. If you find that you haven't lived those values, ask yourself why that is the case and write down ways you think you can live your leadership values better.

For example, one of my values is empathy. One of the ways that I have demonstrated this recently is through a chance encounter I had with an Afghan refugee at our local park. As I was walking my daughters to the park, I noticed a vehicle with an Afghan flag sticker in the window. I had a conversation with this gentleman—whose name is Gharzi—that was facilitated by his 11-year-old son, who interpreted for us. Gharzi and his family—a wife and six kids—fled the Taliban in August 2021. He landed in Minnesota and works nights at Walmart stocking the shelves. Gharzi could not be prouder of his job. It definitely stirred something inside of me as I actively listened to his story. This man did not give me a sad tale of the challenges his family is facing, but I could tell that they were in need as I noticed many of the kids were wearing shoes a few sizes too small. I had my oldest daughter, Hazelyn, run to our house and get some money that we could bless this family with.

Practicing empathy is not about taking on another person's problems, but it's about listening, staying curious, and providing practical help. Gharzi and I exchanged phone numbers and have stayed in touch. As a thank you, his family prepared a feast of traditional Afghan food that was delivered to our house. This has nothing to do with something that happened at work, but it helped me set the example of how I want my daughters to be. They saw how I was proactive in noticing this man and how I listened to him to tell his story. At the same time, Gharzi and his wife similarly modeled empathy for their children in preparing the gift of their traditional food for my family.

All the leadership tips I am sharing in this book are just as applicable in our personal lives as they are in our professional lives. If you're truly living your leadership values, they'll consistently appear in various aspects of your life, regardless of whether your "team" is in your workplace, your community, or your family.

6

Service-Based Leadership

Simply put, service-based leadership is being able to meet the needs of others. It's a philosophy of leading others by serving them. When we meet the needs of others, we help create a culture focused on collaboration with individuals feeling empowered and more engaged, compared to when we lead with a more authoritative approach. There is a plethora of books and research on the topic that highlight many of the benefits of this approach to leadership, including happier employees, reduced turnover, better organizational performance, and more innovation and creativity.

As in the other chapters, I am going to be sharing some stories from my own experiences and from people who have impacted my life. But before we dive in, I want you to take a minute to think of someone who has had a big impact on your life. What specifically has that person done to influence who you are and how you show up as a leader? I would venture to say that the majority of you did not think of your boss. There's nothing wrong if you did—you just might be one of the fortunate few who's had an amazing boss—it's just that in my experience of asking this question, very few have said it was someone who was their boss. Often people will say it was a parent, a teacher, a coach, or maybe even a friend's parent who had the biggest impact on their lives. I was fortunate to find one of these people among my platoon leaders on my first deployment to Afghanistan.

Willingness to Learn

Jon Post was a young lieutenant (LT) in his mid-20s, just a few years out of the United States Military Academy at West Point. At that time, I was 22 years old and a newly promoted sergeant with one combat deployment under my belt. Most LTs in the military get a bad rap—a common saying is that you cannot spell "lost" without "LT." Some might deserve that, but I don't believe in using a broad brush to label everyone.

Jon joined our unit after we got back from Iraq and as we started to train up for our first Afghanistan deployment. I could tell there was something different about this guy, but I just couldn't put my finger on it. First of all, he was a freak of an athlete who runs like a deer. On the weekends he would bike 60 miles in a day just for fun. He understood the importance of taking care of himself and the example that he set for his soldiers.

The typical progression for a newly commissioned field artillery officer is as follows: fire support officer, fire direction officer/ platoon leader, and battery executive officer. Jon had done his time as a fire support officer and was now our platoon leader for our two-gun platoon. The technical skills that made him successful as a fire support officer were going to be much different than the skills needed leading a platoon of two 105mm howitzer cannons.

Unlike other LTs I've served with, Jon was quick to admit what he didn't know. He looked to soldiers in the platoon to help get him up to speed and he asked a lot of questions. This was kind of strange for many of us because we'd never seen an LT ask us to teach him before. But it spoke volumes about his character and his leadership.

Whether you're a team leader like Jon, a corporate head, or a team member, how you adapt to change matters. What's been your approach when technology changes, or you change positions or even industries and there's a learning curve? If you work in a job that is very process-oriented, such as a bank teller, supply-chain coordinator, any type of maintenance technician job, or a myriad of others, you know exactly what I'm talking about. How you did things even a couple of years ago is probably different than how you are doing them today. And it will continue to change. Unfortunately, many people are resistant to change, either because they have an unwillingness to learn something new or they're afraid someone will see their lack of knowledge or skill as a weakness.

There are a lot of things that you could do to be a better service-based leader. But in a situation like what Jon Post found himself in—starting a new position, which you will sometimes find yourself in, too—the ability to be vulnerable, to admit what you don't know, and to ask for help is at the top of the list. Recall that in the previous chapter I said that people mirror the behaviors of others around them. Jon's willingness to ask for help serves as a powerful reminder that it's okay if you don't know everything and emphasizes the importance for you to speak up and ask for help in those situations.

Leading Alongside People

My platoon and I arrived in Afghanistan in early March of 2005 and, as odd as it sounds, it was not fighting season yet. The difficult terrain and weather during the winter and early spring did not make for a conducive environment for military operations—for either side. The vast majority of attacks against us took place after the snow had melted and the weather was more favorable for the enemy fighters, usually April to October.

When we arrived at forward operating base (FOB) Shkin, the gun pit areas were a soggy, muddy mess. Once we had our howitzer cannons set up to fire, our next mission was position improvement—and we had a lot of work to do. We basically had to destroy the setup from the previous unit and start from scratch. This was going to be a lot of physical work. A lot of sandbags would need to be filled. And can you guess who was out there with us many days, shoulder to shoulder, filling the sandbags? That's right, Lieutenant Jon Post, leading from the front and leading by example. He was not the type of leader who would tell someone to do something if he would not do it himself.

Building Authentic Relationships

One of the ways Lieutenant Jon Post embodied the ideals of a service-based leader was that he built authentic relationships with his soldiers. These relationships go deeper than the casual water cooler conversation about the weather. Developing an authentic connection does not mean you need to be best friends and have sleepovers on the weekends. It means you have sincere and transparent communication, along with mutual trust and respect. In these connections, people feel at ease being their authentic selves, freely expressing thoughts and emotions without the fear of judgment. Jon developed these relationships through casual conversations with his soldiers that he would slowly take deeper and deeper. Eventually he would ask us what our goals in life were and how he could help us attain those. For me, that meant being able to finish college, as I mentioned in Chapter 4.

I spent a few weeks at Bagram Airfield for some more medical care after I was wounded. At the end of June, I was finally able to get back out there with my soldiers (a great story in and of itself that I'll talk about in the next chapter). Jon Post was the motivating factor to get me enrolled in the online courses that

I took. But the tricky part was that I needed to have a certified proctor in order to take my exams—someone to basically make sure that I wasn't cheating. Jon filled out the trove of necessary paperwork and played that role for me. But he took it a huge step past that. He spent a significant amount of time and money to actually become credentialed to teach college-credit-level classes to any soldier at our location who wanted them. These were one- or two-credit courses, usually involving military science or leadership that would transfer to accredited academic institutions. I highly doubt that was happening at any other location in Afghanistan at that time.

I experienced firsthand how building authentic relationships can impact a team's performance. Fostering genuine connections with colleagues requires a blend of sincere communication, empathy, and a dedication to cultivating a positive and supportive workplace atmosphere. Here are some actionable tips that you can take to start doing this today:

- **Practice active listening:** We have so many distractions fighting for our attention, and I think we've all been on both sides of this type of conversation at least once: one person is talking, and the other person is lost in their phone. Practice active listening by giving your full attention to your coworkers when they are speaking. Avoid interrupting and show that you value their perspective. And ask questions to ensure you understand their point of view.

- **Show empathy:** Demonstrate empathy by understanding and acknowledging the feelings and experiences of your coworkers. I really like to hit on this one when working with front-line managers and supervisors, especially in those industries where they may not be seen as the most approachable people. Consider, for example, a new employee working on an oil rig. They normally work what is called a hitch: two weeks on and two weeks off with 12-hour shifts. That very first hitch can make their heads spin. I tell these managers and supervisors to think about their first hitch when they came into the industry. Remember what it was like when you first joined an experienced crew. Take new people under your wing and offer them the support and direction they need to be successful; otherwise, you are just setting them up for failure.

- **Share your experiences:** This really goes hand in hand with showing empathy but take it deeper. I love sharing my failures with others. Those are the times where I feel like I have learned the most in my life. Open up about your own experiences and challenges. Sharing personal stories can help create a sense of connection and relatability with your coworkers. Don't be shy about sharing your successes either!

- **Be supportive:** Show up for your coworkers during challenging times. Remember, many people are afraid to ask for help. Go out there and offer it. Maybe an inexperienced employee has been put in charge of their first project. You've been there, you've learned some lessons. Be proactive in problem-solving and collaborative efforts. Let them know they are not alone and that you are a phone call, text, or email away to offer your help.

- **Engage in team-building activities:** In the military we called these "mandatory fun-days," a joke on the formality of it all. But I encourage you to participate in team-building activities or events. These can provide opportunities for informal interactions and bonding. If you are the one planning the event, I encourage you to try to plan it during work hours—we all have commitments outside of work and sometimes those commitments can prevent people from participating, which in turn can make them feel left out. Also, if these are hourly paid employees, you had better pay them for this time as well.

The vast amount of research that has been conducted into what makes a high-performing team successful continues to show the importance of building authentic relationships with our colleagues. That research also shows that the more you know someone, the more likely you are to watch out for them, have their back, and to make sure they are safe. This is even more vitally important for people who are working in high-risk jobs. Again, one more time for those in the back: *You do not need to be best friends with your coworkers.*

Keep in mind that cultivating genuine connections is a continuous journey. Establishing trust and understanding requires time. Your commitment to consistent actions and a sincere concern for your coworkers' welfare plays a very important role in developing authentic workplace relationships.

Having Difficult Conversations

As my military deployment in Afghanistan continued, I got an up-close view on what a true service-based leader looks like in action, not just on paper. Lieutenant Jon Post was the type of guy—and I had seen him do it—who could sit you down and tell you the 12 different ways you sucked at life, but you would leave that conversation with a smile on your face. Why? Because you knew that he cared about you. He wanted to see you succeed. And he would be by you every step of the way, cheering you on, and providing every resource needed in order for you to be successful.

I believe the inability to have difficult conversations with our colleagues is one of the biggest barriers to becoming a truly high-performing team. I've asked a lot of people—literally thousands—why it's hard for them to have tough conversations with their colleagues. The number one answer with a bullet is that they are afraid of how the other person will react. For the most part, we're all pretty nice people and we'd rather avoid the potential for conflict if we can. When we do that, we fail to hold ourselves and others accountable and we create a toxic culture where mediocrity is tolerated.

In addition to shying away from conflict, I've found that most people just haven't been trained to have these types of conversations. And that's not a knock on you if you haven't; I wasn't well equipped to have those conversations either until I learned some great tips from Jon that have helped me better handle these situations:

- **Start with love:** Yep, the big L word. I know it can be pretty scary when talking about our coworkers. But what I mean by starting with love is to recognize your mindset prior to the conversation and remember that you are having that conversation because you care about that person. You want to see them succeed. Keep that mindset throughout the conversation.

- **Be specific:** Focus on what matters and the purpose of the conversation. This might even require some prep work on your end, especially if you're not used to these conversations. It's okay to practice! When you focus on the topic at hand, you can prevent going down unnecessary rabbit holes that are going to get you away from the purpose of your conversation.

- **Focus on behaviors:** A behavior is something you can see or hear, such as someone letting out a sigh or tapping their foot. When you focus on behaviors, it helps make the conversation more objective and cuts down on conflict. For example, if you tell your colleague that you felt they were being rude in the meeting last week, chances are they will get pretty defensive. But if you say, "I noticed you were on the phone for the majority of my presentation. . ." that is a behavior. They can't argue with that.

- **Avoid exaggerated generalities:** Now, I've *never* been guilty of doing that before. See what I did there? If someone is late turning in a report and we tell them they are *always* late, they're going to think of all those times that they weren't late and get defensive. Other common examples include "Millennials are lazy," "Lawyers are dishonest," "Boomers don't understand technology." I could go on and on, but you get my drift.

- **Speak for yourself:** When you talk about the impact someone else's actions have, make sure you speak for yourself, or you at least have the authority to speak for others. If I tell my colleague Jerod that his side conversations in the meeting last week were distracting for everyone, do you know what Jerod will do? He's going to launch an investigation and find someone who could care less that he was having a side conversation and my feedback to him is out the window. In this instance, it would be more beneficial to say, "Jerod, I noticed you were carrying on a side conversation with Brian during the meeting yesterday. That made me feel like you don't respect my time or the effort I put forward." See the difference?

Intimidating People Isn't Leading Them

When you're leading people, be careful not to be the opposite of a service-based leader: someone who tries to lead through fear and intimidation. I rarely saw this type of leadership in the highly structured command and control environment in the military, but I did find it in the civilian world. I had recently started a new job and was on one of my first weekly team calls. During the discussion, I casually mentioned the possibility of taking a day off the following month to participate in a charity golf event for Tee It Up for the Troops. Prior to joining the organization, I had been informed multiple times about the company's policy of unlimited time off—just put it on the calendar, they said. Taking this at face value, I shared my plans during the team call, intending to provide a heads-up.

To my surprise, immediately after the team call, my boss called me directly and conveyed concerns, stating that they might have made a mistake in hiring me. It would have been one thing to tell me that the company's written policy didn't reflect the current culture and to explain that I'd need to adjust my expectations to the existing reality. But suggesting I shouldn't have been hired because I was following actual company policy was something else altogether. This sentiment persisted, with my boss later suggesting, on multiple occasions, that it might be time for me to begin a professional wind-down at the company. This is also the person who was notorious for calling colleagues very early in the morning to give them an earful on something they did wrong.

Leading through fear and intimidation usually gets you minimal compliance and a fixed mindset, but when you lead through influence you get discretionary effort and help cultivate a growth mindset. When people are led through fear and intimidation, they're less likely to feel safe being proactive, and they're less likely to be emotionally invested to do so. But service-based leadership motivates and inspires people to pour their energy into developing themselves and the organization in a productive way.

Service-based leadership is important because it helps create a positive workplace atmosphere, improves employee well-being, and plays a key role in the enduring success and sustainability of organizations. By placing a premium on serving others, leaders can cultivate resilient, collaborative teams driven to attain shared objectives.

Your Challenge

Go out to lunch with a colleague and get to know them on a deeper level. Try not to talk about work. Some great questions to help you spark conversation include:

- What's the first vehicle you owned?
- What was your first job?
- Tell me about your hometown.
- What is an accomplishment outside of your professional career that you're most proud of?

Go start building those authentic relationships—they make a difference!

7

Motivating Others

Do you ever have those days when you're on your way to work and you just feel like you're on top of the world and ready to tackle anything that gets in your way? What about those days where you have absolutely zero desire to get anything accomplished? I am almost certain everyone will say yes to both questions—we've all experienced both. It's unrealistic to think we can have the pep-band blasting out our favorite "Jock Jams" songs in our head all day (shoutout to those of you who get that '90s reference).

The first part of this chapter is going to look at motivation, and I will share with you my experiences with one leader specifically and how he motivated those around him. I'll also share some specific practices on what we can do as leaders to better motivate those around us. In the second part of the chapter, I'll share how an international event in 2021 spoke to my values and motivated me to take action.

What Is Motivation?

At its core, motivation is what drives a person to do something. At the most basic level, it's the force that makes us act to make sure our basic needs are met—food, water, shelter, survival—that type of thing. When we get past having our basic needs met, what motivates me may not motivate you, and vice versa. We are all unique, and as leaders it's important to understand the needs of our people and to ensure we tailor our motivational strategies to the individual.

The ability to motivate ourselves and others has long been a topic of study and research by very smart people. I've became quite interested in the art and science behind motivation after I read the book *Drive* by Daniel Pink. If you're looking for a great read to highlight some of the research that has taken place, I cannot recommend that book enough. There are also several great videos of Daniel Pink talking about motivation—find those and watch them.

In this chapter, we'll explore some real-world examples of different motivational strategies, both for motivating ourselves and for motivating others.

Meet Greg

In Chapter 1, I talked about the challenges of showing up as a new soldier in an Army airborne unit. It's basically a rite of passage for a new soldier to go through some good old-fashioned "smoking" when arriving at a new unit. "Smoking" is a term used in the military to describe rigorous physical exercise or drills as a means of disciplinary measure or improving physical fitness and endurance. I certainly experienced my fair share and admittedly have been on the other side of the coin greeting new soldiers when they arrive. I assure you, it was all above board and no one was ever harmed—just lots of pushups and burpees.

I remember after one intense smoke session, I was feeling pretty defeated and second-guessing a lot of my decisions. That's when Sergeant Greg Trent gave me a little pep talk. Greg held a position in a different section, in a different platoon, so it was a little strange for him to come to me, but once you knew Greg you realized that was pretty much his standard operating procedure. He wasn't going to let invisible barriers stop him from mentoring young soldiers. He was different from most noncommissioned officers (sergeants and above of the enlisted ranks). He wasn't the kind who was going to yell and rant and rave; he had a much more sophisticated approach that I found really resonated with many soldiers.

As he sat next to me, Greg reminded me not to take it personally. He shared the story of what he went through when he arrived at his first unit in the 82nd Airborne Division. He didn't feel sorry for me, and he didn't make excuses, but what he did was listen to me, challenge me to shift my perspective, and remind me that it gets better. Greg knew that motivating others was about finding out what their needs were (at the time, I just needed someone to listen to me), meeting those needs, and then challenging them to take action. From then on, I knew Greg would be a person I could turn to if I ever needed someone to listen and give advice.

Greg and I deployed as part of the same artillery battery once to Iraq and once to Afghanistan. When we returned from our deployment to Iraq, Greg submitted his paperwork to apply for Special Forces. As part of that process, a soldier must complete a grueling three-work course called Special Forces Assessment and Selection, or Selection for short. It's a tryout to basically get invited to actually attend the Special Forces Qualification Course—commonly referred to as Q Course. Selection is designed to assess a candidate's physical fitness, mental toughness, and ability to work effectively in small teams. Soldiers participate in a variety of physically challenging activities, land navigation exercises, and team-oriented events. This course is difficult enough just to complete, and most don't finish. But even if you do finish, it doesn't guarantee you get selected to move forward to the Q Course. Of course, Greg completed and was selected— just as we knew he would.

Getting Back in the Fight

Our unit was gearing up to deploy to Afghanistan, and we all assumed Greg would not be with us because he was waiting on his assignment for the Q Course. But Greg made the decision to give up his slot for Q Course and to deploy with our unit to Afghanistan. He could have easily chosen not to deploy, and no one would have thought less of him. But that's just not the type of person he was.

I was sent to Bagram Airfield for further medical treatment after I was wounded. Greg was stationed with our headquarters element of our unit at Bagram Airfield, in charge of ensuring all of our ammunition was getting out to the platoons. Greg made it a point to stop by every day to make sure I was okay. But I have to be honest, I was scared to get back out there and get in the fight. Two soldiers who had been standing next to me had just been killed and eight of us were wounded. I was having nightmares and could barely sleep. The images replayed in my head every day.

I didn't want others to know I was scared. I was a sergeant, a paratrooper, I'd been to Iraq. We're not supposed to be scared, right? Of course, I was wrong. I don't think I would have been able to continue on that deployment if not for Greg and a conversation we had. A few weeks after being at Bagram Airfield, Greg asked if I was ready to get back out there with my soldiers. He could see the apprehension in my eyes. He knew how I felt. He sat there and he listened to me as I laid out my worries before him. He didn't judge me. Greg recognized that my need at the time was for someone to listen to me and to validate my concerns. As we spoke, we also talked about his potential career in the Special Forces and his decision to forego the Q Course so he could deploy with us again. That example spoke volumes to me and showed me what my presence could do for my soldiers to see me again.

Technically, I was not medically cleared to be back out there with my soldiers. As mentioned in Chapter 5, I still had stitches that prevented me from wearing my body armor, which precluded me from actively contributing to our mission supporting the Special Forces soldiers through indirect fire. But Greg came to the rescue. After our conversation, I felt motivated to get back out there. I could not imagine what our platoon was going through after those events. I knew they were in the thick of it as I heard the reports—they were firing every day out there. The attack on June 8 basically kicked off the fighting season for us. Since Greg was in charge of making sure the ammunition got out to the platoons, he had some pull with the folks running the helicopter manifests. To this day, I am not 100% sure how he did it, but he got me on a flight and got me back out with my soldiers.

Upon completion of our deployment to Afghanistan, Greg left and successfully completed the Special Forces Q School and earned his Green Beret—as we knew he would. He went on to serve numerous deployments to Afghanistan with his Special Forces unit. On July 31, 2012, Greg was shot while on patrol with his unit. Unfortunately, he succumbed to his wounds on August 8. A few weeks later, many of us from our unit gathered at Arlington National Cemetery and laid Greg to rest. He is gone but never forgotten. His wife, Beth, continues to honor his legacy through the amazing work she does supporting other Gold Star families. The cost of freedom is buried in the ground.

The way Greg interacted with me and everyone else was like offering a master class in motivation. When I needed someone to listen, he made himself available. When I was unsure and afraid, he offered me support and encouragement. He showed me that true leaders show up for their people and take care of them. He led by example with his dedication to his career growth and development, but he was also willing to place his commitment to his people above his own needs. And he inspired me to want to do the same. The world needs more motivational leaders like Greg.

Intrinsic Motivation and Extrinsic Motivation

There are two sources of motivation—intrinsic and extrinsic. Extrinsic motivation comes from external rewards—like getting your paycheck, commission bonuses, profit sharing, and so on. I'm not going to argue—most of us are not coming in to work if we're not getting paid. And there are other ways to recognize people with external rewards, some of which I will talk about in Chapter 11. I'm sure we'd all love to give people a raise, but we know that's not feasible. But if we want to build a more sustainable level of motivation, we need to look at the intrinsic factors, just like Greg did.

Remember, we are all unique, and what motivates you is different than what motivates me. Get to know people and find out what it is that gets them excited to do the work. With that in mind, here are some ways you can motivate others that will cost you zero dollars:

- **Inspire a sense of purpose:** Establish a connection between the tasks at hand and a broader, meaningful purpose. In Chapter 1 we talked about discovering your purpose; now let's help others discover theirs! Assist people in recognizing the profound impact their contributions can have on the team, organization, or society. Sometimes it's great to remind people of the good your team or organization is doing. Maybe you work for an electric company—you literally help keep the lights on. That's pretty purposeful work. Or you work for an environmental services company and remind employees that maybe the work isn't always glamourous, but it is something that serves a greater purpose in our world. Later in this chapter, I'm going to share how a sense of purpose inspired me to take action.

- **Provide challenging work:** When I ask people one of the things they love about their job, many people say they love the challenge of the work. Encourage people to focus on mastering their skills that make them successful at work. The pursuit of excellence, personal growth, and sense of accomplishing challenging tasks can be intrinsically motivating for many people. I've been fortunate to work with a lot of great construction companies, and it's always fun to see them in action when they are faced with a new challenge—everything from a delivery of materials not arriving on time to a massive change order on their projects. You can tell the people who love a good challenge.

- **Encourage autonomy:** Dan Pink talks a lot about our desire to be self-directed. Strive to help provide individuals with autonomy and the ability to make decisions related to their work. Allowing them to have control and ownership over their tasks can help them be more motivated. In the military, many things are pretty black and white. But the best leaders find opportunities for people to have autonomy, even in the most straightforward tasks. For example, when you have a task you need someone to do, let them know what the constraints are, what the standard is, and let them go. You might be very surprised at what people are capable of when given the right amount of autonomy.

- **Create a positive work environment:** No one likes going in to work if it's a depressing environment full of negative people. Cultivate a positive and inclusive workplace culture. A supportive environment where individuals feel valued, respected, and encouraged can naturally help someone feel more motivated. I've seen firsthand how a negative person can have an outsized impact on those around them. In one of the first sessions when I was conducting some training with a company, a person said that he calls his guys idiots all the time and that they don't mind. He told me it motivates them. Of course, my next training was with that group of people, and they talked about how demoralizing that person was on their self-esteem and how he created a culture of fear. But they were scared to speak up to him and so were others in the company. Remember, if you lead through fear and intimidation, you might get compliance but that's about it. You will not get that discretionary effort that is a hallmark of a high-performing team.

- **Encourage creativity and innovation:** This goes hand-in-hand with encouraging autonomy. Help others find opportunities to explore and implement creative ideas. Allowing room for innovation and creative problem-solving can stimulate intrinsic motivation in others. Google is a great example of an organization that had done several things to promote creativity and innovation in the past, including innovation workshops where employees gather to share ideas and create new ones; hackathons, which are organized opportunities for employees to work on projects they are passionate about; and radical collaboration, which brings together a widely diverse group to develop new projects, such as having someone from the facilities staff, someone from marketing, someone from engineering, and someone from sales all in a room to provide their unique perspectives on products and services. However, they have also provided a strong case study in how people react when that culture is changed due to leadership turnover. I've found that when we work with the same people all the time, we tend to all think alike and come up with the same ideas. But when we get a diverse group of people together, each with their own unique perspective, they're not afraid to ask that question others might think is stupid—which could very well be the key to unlocking new ideas.

A lot of people will argue that money is an effective motivator. As I mentioned earlier, not many people are going to go in to work if they know they will not be paid. But let me ask you this: if I double what you are making right now, will it magically make you a better employee? Will more money increase your performance? Before you rush to nod your head and say "yep," consider this: Is your actual performance going to increase, or are you just going to show up earlier and stay later and feel like you are doing more work? A motivator for showing up and putting in time isn't as strong as other motivators for truly performing at a higher level.

Driven by Values

As I've studied motivation and reflected on my own experiences, I am always intrigued by people who do things for others even though there is no extrinsic reward involved. This could be someone who volunteers at the local animal shelter taking dogs on walks, someone who volunteers their time and raises money for a favorite charitable organization, or those who pitch in to clean up after natural disasters. What I've found is that when we tie the work to our personal values, people will do tremendous things.

The United States military had begun to withdraw their troops and equipment from Afghanistan in May 2021, with a deadline of August 31 to be out of the country. By the middle of August, the Taliban had regained control of most of the country from the fleeing Afghan National Army and were marching on Kabul, the capital city. At this point, I was no longer actively serving in the military and had transitioned to civilian life in Minnesota. On August 14, I sent a message to my former interpreter Ali Shah that simply stated, "Are you safe?" Little did I know that this one message would lead to many nights of little sleep as I worked to help him and his family evacuate Afghanistan as the Taliban took over.

The military was consolidated at Kabul International Airport and were working frantically to evacuate military personnel, American citizens, and Afghan civilians who had supported the coalition forces. The idea of having to live under the Taliban regime scared many Afghans and rightfully so. Tens of thousands of them flocked to the airport in Kabul desperately hoping to get on one of the limited evacuation flights. Many of us saw the images as innocent Afghan civilians overtook the runway and literally clung for life to the departing aircraft—willing to risk everything to leave the country they love due to the Taliban. The US military were able to regain control of the airport and were trying their best to get as many people as they could out of the country.

As Ali Shah and I began to message back and forth, I thought about my own family and the lengths I would go to protect them. I also viewed this as an opportunity to make a difference and

I knew that I had to do something to help him, his wife, and his five kids get out of the country. But what could I do from my small town in Minnesota to make this happen? I wasn't quite sure, but I wasn't going to quit until I had exhausted every option.

I also had a business to run, I had clients to take care of, and a family to provide for. This wasn't going to pay bills or put food on the table. But it was so much bigger than that. I felt this immense motivation stirring inside of me—a surge of adrenaline I hadn't felt since being in Afghanistan, and it seemed to last forever as I worked my connections to help Ali Shah and his family escape what would be certain death at the hands of the Taliban due to his work with the US military.

I sat right here at my desk where I am writing this right now and reached out to everyone I had previously served with to see if we knew any US military personnel who were in the country. All the while I tried to reassure Ali Shah that everything was going to be okay. I felt an obligation to do everything in my power to help him because he had sacrificed so much to help us. As the Taliban retook Kabul, Ali Shah was sleeping in a different location every night. I was not the only veteran trying to help their interpreter get out of the country. There were literally thousands of us hard at work—many taking vacation time from work to help the cause. I highly encourage you to read *Operation Pineapple Express*, which tells the story of retired Special Forces Lieutenant Colonel Scott Mann and his mission to evacuate former Afghan Special Forces soldiers and their families.

I was finally able to get a direct connection to someone on the ground at the airport in Kabul. Paul Orduno was a soldier who was on every deployment with me. He was now an Apache helicopter pilot and was piloting one of the Apaches that cleared the runway for the giant C-17 aircraft to take off with Afghans clinging to the wheel. Paul was an invaluable resource and helped me connect with other resources who were very helpful.

Through modern technology, I was able to help Ali Shah and his family navigate past Taliban checkpoints and arrive to the airport. But it was extreme chaos at the airport; people had been there for days desperately trying to get out. After two dangerous trips to the airport and two failed attempts, I told Ali Shah that he needed to take his family one more time and be prepared to stay there for an indeterminate amount of time—no running water, no hot food, no showers, none of the daily amenities many of us take for granted. Again, this is a young mother and father and five children under the age of 12.

I reassured Ali Shah that I would not give up, but his chances were bleak. On the inside, I tried to ready my heart for the inevitable failure that was going to happen and how I would process it. Somehow, Ali Shah remained upbeat and confident. It motivated me not to give up. My wife, Shanna, provided great support and was equally invested in the outcome. As I worked around the clock, I became aware of numerous threats of violence against the crowds at the airport. Ali Shah and his family were stationed right outside of Abby Gate, a small entrance to the airport separated by a canal of sewage that smelled exactly like you think it would.

Despite several failed attempts, we persisted. And on August 25 Ali Shah and his family were helped across the canal thanks to the heroic effort by Thomas Richardson, a former US Army Ranger who was now working as a contractor in Afghanistan. Less than 24 hours after making it into the airport, a suicide bomber detonated at Abby Gate, and 13 American military members were killed, along with hundreds of innocent Afghans. The canal ran red with the blood of the victims.

Even after leaving Afghanistan, Ali Shah's journey to freedom was not complete. It would take several months, with stops in Qatar, Germany, and a military installation in New Jersey before they were finally resettled. In March of 2022, I saw Ali Shah for the first time in person since I left Afghanistan in 2008. It has been an inspiration to watch him and his family flourish in his new country.

But our work was not done. We still had about a week before the deadline for withdrawal. I was riding a high of emotions and offered my time to others who were trying to get people out. I was soon contacted by another former soldier who was trying to get his former interpreter out of the country. This one was different; it involved several young kids who were American citizens. Their father was a former interpreter and had successfully immigrated to the United States several years prior and the kids were born in the United States. At the time the Taliban took over, the family was visiting relatives in Afghanistan. I guided them on the phone to a remote gate being guarded by some Afghans and American contractors. The kids were all American citizens, but their mother was not. If I was not able to keep them together, they might never see their mom again.

I was on a video call with the family as they braved warning shots fired by the Afghans working at the gate. It was chaos, and I had no idea what was going on. They somehow managed to hand the phone to the American contractor working the gate. He had no reason to take that phone from them. But he did and we had a short conversation; my wife actually videoed this in real time. If you ever see me in person, I'd love to show you. I told him I had shed blood in that country, and it would mean everything to me if he could help them get to safety. After a short pause, he replied, "You got my word, they'll get in." I still don't know that gentleman's name, but that family and I are forever grateful to him. I have kept in touch with this family to this day and enjoy seeing them build a successful life in the United States.

How Motivation Works

People often want to reduce motivation to a couple of positive-energy phrases. Those are great, but they don't provide deeper motivation. Think about how the previous section's stories about evacuation from Afghanistan tie to the intrinsic motivators:

- **Inspire a sense of purpose:** My military leaders and the many Afghan soldiers, translators, and civilians all inspired in me a desire to help the people of Afghanistan have better lives. When the days of the evacuation came, that inspiration motivated me to help both the Afghans I'd worked with and those I'd never met.

- **Provide challenging work:** Throughout the evacuation effort, everyone was challenged by the danger, logistics, limited resources, and timetable. But so many people rose to the challenge and worked together to help as many people as possible.

- **Encourage autonomy:** I was in Minnesota. I was able to speak with people in Afghanistan on the phone, but ultimately Ali Shah, Apache helicopter pilot Paul Orduno, former US Army Ranger Thomas Richardson, and countless others were motivated to take autonomous steps and think outside the box to help people.

- **Create a positive work environment:** The relationships I developed with my military and Afghan contacts when I had been stationed in Afghanistan had created such a positive work environment that I was motivated to jump in and do what I could, even when I was in Minnesota. And Ali Shah and I worked with each other to keep our spirits up throughout the whole evacuation experience.

- **Encourage creativity and innovation:** I reached out and shared with a contractor I'd never met that I'd been injured in Afghanistan. I have no idea what he had to do that day to save the family I was trying to help, but I put my trust in him, and I'm sure he was creative and innovative in getting that family to safety.

You don't need to be a Green Beret badass or help someone escape a terrorist group to motivate others. These are just experiences from my own personal journey. You can help spark a fire in others that will motivate them to accomplish great things. The key is to get to know people and find what gets them excited about the work they do. The job market can fluctuate but people are more than capable of going down the road to get a paycheck from someone else. Find out what attracted them to that job in the first place. Connect their work to the bigger picture. And challenge them along the way. You got this!

Your Challenge

My wife introduced me to the idea of a vision board. I challenge you to conduct a vision board workshop within your organization. This exercise not only helps individuals to clarify their own goals but also creates a supportive community where they can motivate each other. It taps into the power of visualization and goal setting, fostering a sense of purpose and inspiration. This exercise will be described for an in-person workshop using physical materials, but it could easily be adapted to work online with virtual resources.

Here is what you need to do:

1. **Introduction (10 minutes):** Begin by explaining the purpose of the exercise—to help individuals visualize and set goals for their future. Highlight the significance of possessing a well-defined vision as a catalyst for motivation.

2. **Materials (5 minutes):** Provide each participant with a piece of poster board, magazines, scissors, glue, and markers. Encourage them to bring personal photos or any other items they find inspiring.

3. **Reflective Exercise (15 minutes):** Ask participants to reflect on their personal and professional goals. What do they want to achieve in the short term and long term? What inspires them? Have them write this down on a sheet of paper.

4. **Collage Creation (30 minutes):** Instruct participants to flip through magazines and find images, words, or phrases that represent their goals and aspirations. They will cut these out and arrange them on their vision boards. Encourage them to be creative!

5. **Show and Tell (20 minutes):** After completing their vision boards, ask participants to share their creations with the group. This can be done in pairs or small groups, depending on the size of the audience. Participants should explain the significance of the images and words they chose. Don't forget to share yours as well.

6. **Goal Setting (10 minutes):** Facilitate a discussion on how participants can break down their vision into actionable steps. Remember the SMART goals from Chapter 4? Encourage them to set specific, measurable, achievable, relevant, and time-bound (SMART) goals based on their vision boards.

7. **Accountability Partners (10 minutes):** Pair participants or create small groups and assign them as accountability partners. Encourage them to check in with each other periodically to discuss progress, share challenges, and provide support.

8. **Closing and Reflection (10 minutes):** Wrap up the workshop by emphasizing the importance of staying motivated and focused on their goals. Encourage participants to contemplate the lessons they've gained and consider how they can integrate these newfound insights into their everyday experiences.

8

The Art of Delegation

When I engage with leaders in the organizations I work with, a common theme appears. Many of them express a genuine desire to invest more time in connecting with their teams, yet they find themselves tied to their desks due to an overwhelming workload. When I inquire about the possibility of delegation, two consistent responses emerge: I don't trust anyone else, or I don't have the time teach someone else.

Delegation is the process of entrusting tasks, responsibilities, or decision-making authority to individuals within a team or organization. Leaders who effectively delegate help distribute the workload, empower team members, and ensure that tasks are completed efficiently. Effective delegation involves assigning the right tasks to the right people based on their skills and capabilities, providing clear instructions and expectations, and maintaining accountability to ensure successful outcomes.

I have found that delegation is an art—it's much more nuanced than just divvying up the work and assigning people tasks. It requires a leader to be intuitive, adaptable, and have a deep understanding of the strengths and challenges of their team. Like any form of art, it involves creativity, finesse, and a commitment to continual improvement. From my experiences, it is a crucial skill that separates someone from just being a high performer to a person capable of leading high-performing teams.

Delegating to Grow

On my last deployment to Afghanistan, I was a squad leader. Our platoon fancied ourselves as the most versatile platoon in the Army due to the ever-changing missions we were tasked with. The last 7 months of our 15-month deployment were spent conducting border control operations near the Pakistani border. Essentially, I was tasked with leading my squad on a mission every other day. At this time I also knew that I was going to be leaving the Army, but I often found myself wondering if I had done enough for my soldiers to carry on the mission once I was gone. As I reflect on that today, I feel a little embarrassment at my bravado; the Army would continue with or without me, just as the sun will continue to rise in the east. However, I was invested in the development of my soldiers and their success was important to me.

Prior to every mission, I would lead a pre-mission briefing, just as you may have a shift change meeting, job safety analysis, or project update briefing prior to the start of your workday. In this briefing, I would cover the pertinent information regarding the mission: what the mission was; the route we were taking; what the intelligence reports said; the number of personnel, weapons, and vehicles; how we would respond to enemy contact; and any contingency plans. We also had a scaled-down mockup of the area of operations with little matchbox cars to represent our vehicles. I would use these as visuals as I went through my briefing. Much of this information was pretty standard and did not change much from mission to mission. But I should note that it's important to not get too routine when operating in a combat environment because it makes it much easier for your enemies to target you if you take the same route at the same time every day.

After a few months of running missions, I eventually found myself and my soldiers not engaged in the briefing. "Complacency kills" was a common saying during my time in the Army and I knew

I had a problem on my hands. I would even ask questions at the end of the briefing, but eventually that became too routine. I could spout off all the information in my sleep and started to feel like I was just going through the motions. I saw this as a perfect opportunity not only as a way to help reengage myself and my soldiers in this important briefing but also as a huge opportunity for my soldiers to step up and learn something new.

The day before every mission, I would select one of my soldiers to lead that briefing. When you do something like this, you want to set someone up for success, so you don't want to tell them five minutes prior to a meeting that they're going to be leading it. Give people time to prepare. Leading this briefing was something new for each of my soldiers, so I made sure I took the time to go through every part with them. Even though we all knew each other really well, when it came to their time for the briefing, each briefing leader was pretty nervous. I made it a point to stand right next to them for two main reasons: to help them in case they needed a lifeline, and because it was ultimately still my responsibility to ensure all the information was covered and correct. Some of my soldiers did better than others. But for all of them, it was a huge opportunity to step up and do something different that would benefit their growth and development and get them, and me, reengaged in the work.

Why Delegate?

I've been in many organizations where I've witnessed how a lack of effectively being able to delegate leads to a decrease in production, unengaged employees, and for those working in high-risk industries, a higher propensity for safety incidents. The art of delegation is essential for effective team leadership for several compelling reasons:

- **Optimal resource utilization:** Delegation enables the distribution of tasks based on team members' skills and expertise, ensuring that resources are utilized efficiently. This results in a more productive and capable team.

- **Development of team members:** Delegating tasks allows team members to step up and do something different. Even if it is something that seems very routine to you, such as creating a PowerPoint slide updating the progress of a project, it can be an awesome opportunity for someone else to do something they've never done before. This can help your team members enhance their skills, learn new competencies, and broaden their experience, contributing to their long-term growth.

- **Focus on strategic priorities:** When routine tasks are delegated, it allows leaders the time to concentrate on strategic planning, decision-making, and high-level responsibilities. I often hear from leaders that they wish they could spend more time with their people. The second thing I most often hear is how they wish they had more time to think strategically. Delegating provides you a great opportunity to free up some time to do just that.

- **Empowerment and motivation:** The story I shared earlier in this chapter happened when we were roughly halfway through a long and difficult 15-month deployment. Being able to keep up morale and keeping my soldiers motivated was challenging. I found an additional benefit of delegating also empowered my soldiers by entrusting them with important tasks. This led to a greater sense of accountability, higher morale, and increased motivation.

- **Time management:** Leading a team often comes with numerous challenges and responsibilities that can cause tight time constraints. The art of delegation is a fundamental time management skill for leaders. I mentioned one of the responses I often hear about why people don't delegate is because they don't have the time. Of course, what they fail to realize is that time invested up front in teaching someone a new task will pay dividends in the future. As a leader, when you invest that time upfront in training and empowering team members, you help set the stage for long-term success and increased overall productivity.

These are just a few of the benefits of being able to lead teams when you delegate effectively. It also helps enhance team communication and collaboration, fosters a culture of growth and empowerment, prevents burnout and stress, and allows you the opportunity to increase your role and responsibilities in an organization. It's easy to see the benefits of delegating, but it does come with some very legitimate challenges.

Challenges to Delegating

It can be frustrating to have someone look at all of the work you need to get done and say, "Come on, just delegate to someone else!" It's not that easy, I get it. Personally, I've experienced one of the biggest challenges many leaders face when it comes to delegation but that may be hard to admit: the loss of control.

I remember many challenges that I faced as a college student after my time in the Army, specifically when it came to group work. I was 26 years old when I went back to college after being out in the world with a full-time career—the definition of a nontraditional student. I was very focused on my academic coursework, and I found that many of the other students were just as focused on their social lives as they were their academic lives. There is nothing wrong with that; in fact, one of the best benefits of college is the whole experience of living the college lifestyle. But the differences in regard to the priority of our schoolwork—specifically in group projects—was very challenging, to say the least. I had a fear of losing control over the results of group projects that could impact my academic standing, which in turn could potentially impact my scholarships, my GI Bill benefits, and my professional career. Because of this, I found myself doing all the work. I basically delegated everything to myself. That's not effective delegation.

What is something that you are responsible for at work that you would be concerned about delegating? Many leaders may fear that delegating certain tasks relinquishes control over the outcomes, leading to concerns about quality, efficiency, or alignment with organizational goals.

Imagine you were just promoted from site manager to regional manager. You went from being very hands-on at one site to now being responsible for seven different sites. Your previous site might have a special place in your heart and you may feel that strong desire and even obligation to be very hands-on and in the details, just as you previously were. You're concerned that the new manager is going to undo all your hard work. But what you're actually doing is hindering the new site manager from establishing themselves at the location because you still want the control. You also probably aren't giving enough attention to the other six sites. You can overcome these problems by fostering a culture of trust, providing clear expectations, and maintaining open communication channels. Delegation isn't just about assigning tasks to people. It also includes empowering them to more actively and successfully fulfill the entire range of responsibilities that can be managed in their role.

Another challenge that I've seen prevent leaders from effectively delegating is they just don't know which tasks are right to delegate and which ones are not. I have found it most beneficial to focus on delegating routine or specialized tasks where others can excel and where it is safe for them to fail. Some of my soldiers did really badly when they were giving their first precombat briefing, but it was a huge learning opportunity for them, and most of them improved with time and effort. Keep in mind that you can't expect immediate perfection when delegating. But with a little oversight and support, your team can thrive with delegated tasks. I look back on moments in my life, and the times I failed are often the times I learned the most.

A great strategy is to conduct an analysis of tasks, considering their complexity, the skills that are required, and the importance of each task. You'll look at the process of effective delegation in the next section. Then you'll get a chance at the end of the chapter to think about which tasks you might want to analyze.

How to Delegate Effectively

The art of delegation is a multifaceted skill that requires a strategic approach, clear communication, and an understanding of both tasks and team dynamics. In this section, I'm going to walk you through a process for delegation that I learned at Warrior Leaders Course (WLC) during my time in the military. At the time, WLC was three weeks long and was a requirement to be promoted to the rank of sergeant. It included classroom instruction and hands-on performance training, and culminated in a situational training exercise. Over time, I've modified the process that I learned into what you will see in the next couple of pages. This process consists of task analysis, team member selection, communication, and resource provision.

Analyzing Tasks

The first step in the delegation process involves an analysis of tasks to determine which are suitable for delegating. This step is critical for ensuring that responsibilities are assigned in a manner that not only optimizes efficiency and leverages the strengths of the team but also identifies opportunities for growth and development.

1. Identifying Tasks Suitable for Delegation Not all tasks are created equal, and identifying those that can be delegated is a skill in itself. Routine, time-consuming, and specialized tasks often make great candidates for delegation. However, you need to carefully consider the nature of the task and its impact on overall goals.

2. Assessing Complexity and Importance Assessing the complexity and importance of tasks is crucial for making informed delegation decisions. Tasks that are routine but essential may be suitable for delegation, while complex strategic decisions will often require the leader's direct involvement. Striking a balance between complexity and importance ensures that tasks are appropriately distributed.

Choosing the Right Team Members

Once you've identified the tasks you want to delegate, the next step is selecting the right team members to carry them out. This involves evaluating individual strengths and weaknesses, aligning tasks with skills, and promoting a cohesive team dynamic.

1. Evaluating Strengths and Weaknesses Understanding the strengths and weaknesses of team members is a hallmark function of a good team leader and is fundamental to effective delegation. This assessment goes beyond technical skills and includes factors such as communication style, work preferences, and problem-solving abilities.

2. Matching Tasks with the Right Person Successful delegation involves aligning tasks with individual skills and interests while also identifying areas for others to grow and develop. This not only optimizes performance but also fosters a sense of job satisfaction, engagement, and motivation among team members.

Communicating Clearly

Effective delegation hinges on clear communication. Leaders must adeptly express expectations, goals, and outcomes, establishing open channels for feedback and clarification.

1. Conveying Expectations and Desired Outcomes Delegating tasks begins with being able to convey your expectations. You need to articulate the scope of the task, desired outcomes, and any specific guidelines or standards. This clarity ensures that team members have a good understanding of their responsibilities.

2. Establishing Open Lines of Communication for Feedback
Communication is a two-way street. Leaders must not only convey expectations but also create an environment where team members feel comfortable providing feedback. Open lines of communication help to foster collaboration, allowing for the exchange of ideas, a safe environment to ask questions, and continuous improvement in the delegation process.

Providing Resources and Support

Delegating tasks goes hand in hand with providing the necessary resources and support. Leaders must ensure that delegated tasks have the required resources and offer guidance when needed, creating an environment conducive to success.

1. Ensuring Delegated Tasks Are Supported by the Necessary Resources Delegating a task without providing the required resources sets the stage for failure. Leaders must ensure their team members have access to tools, information, and any other resources essential for the successful completion of the task. This proactive approach prevents bottlenecks and ensures a smooth workflow.

2. Offering Guidance and Support When Needed Delegating does not mean abandoning responsibility. You are not abdicating your responsibility. Leaders are still accountable for the success of the tasks they delegate. Offering guidance and support when team members encounter challenges demonstrates commitment to their success. Whether it's troubleshooting issues or providing additional information, leaders play a pivotal role in ensuring task success.

In essence, delegation is a cornerstone of effective leadership, allowing leaders to harness the collective capabilities of their team, nurture a positive work culture, and guide the organization toward sustained success. Delegation is not just about distributing tasks; it is a strategic leadership tool that contributes to organizational effectiveness, employee development, and the overall success of a team or company. Leaders who master the art of delegation are better positioned to navigate complex challenges and lead their teams to achieve shared goals.

Your Challenge

Time for you to take a shot at doing a task analysis. Make a list of all the tasks that you do in one week. Some examples might include a routine personnel report, answering emails, updating a weekly project tracker, or anything else you regularly deal with. Conduct an analysis of these tasks and see which ones might be suitable for you to delegate to one of your team members. Don't have team members? Make the list anyway—it's a great exercise in understanding and identifying the opportunities that you might be able to delegate and will help prepare you for that time when you do have a team.

As an example to help you out, I came up with my own list of tasks. Please note that I am a one-person operation right now, so I don't have any employees, but I found this is to be a helpful exercise for determining if I want to hire someone and how

I might free up some of my time and energy if I decide to grow my business. Here are a few of my tasks:

1. Task: Responding to Routine Emails

   Delegate: Yes

   Comment: Routine emails are okay to delegate to an assistant.

2. Task: Strategic Planning for Next Year

   Delegate: No

   Comment: I am the key decision-maker at this time but if I had a partner(s) it would be something to explore.

3. Task: Travel and Logistics

   Delegate: Yes

   Comment: This is definitely something that would be helpful for me and free up time for me to focus more strategically on my business.

4. Task: Conducting Marketing Activities

   Delegate: Yes—and I've done it.

   Comment: I've partnered with a great marketing group that has been very helpful in getting the word out there about my business. When I first started my business, I knew marketing was important, but I had no idea what to do. It was the first large investment and one of the best decisions I made in my business.

5. Task: Virtual Meeting with a Prospective Client

   Delegate: No

   Comment: At this point, it's very important that I meet with potential clients because I believe it allows them an opportunity to get to know me and my message. This could definitely change if my business was to grow. I could have someone conduct the initial contact with prospective clients to qualify them as a good fit for the work that I do.

6. Task: Troubleshooting IT Issues

   Delegate: Yes

   Comment: I've already had to do this for issues that were beyond my skill level.

7. Task: Creating Social Media Content

   Delegate: Yes

   Comment: Content creation for social media can be delegated to individuals with marketing or creative expertise.

Leading the Culture

In Part II, we talked about effectively leading teams by leading by example, motivating others, and delegating. In Part III, I'm still going to provide you with more stories from my experiences along with practical tips, but the focus will shift to how we can do that in a way that helps you lead the culture in your organization. What does leading the culture mean? It's how we influence and shape the values, beliefs, behaviors, and overall atmosphere within an organization. Shaping culture isn't exclusive to those in positions of authority like the CEO or vice presidents; it can also be led by individuals at various levels within an organization. Let's jump in.

PART

Leading the Culture

9

Creating a Culture of Accountability

I've learned a few really hard lessons in accountability that I am going to share with you in this chapter. These experiences were not the proudest moments of my life, but they've served as great examples of not only what we can do as individuals to be more accountable, but also how we can shape the culture of accountability in our organizations through our behaviors.

A culture of accountability refers to an organizational environment where individuals take responsibility for their actions, decisions, and performance. In such a culture, there is a shared understanding that each person is held responsible for their duties and obligations, and there are clear expectations regarding performance and behavior. This culture is characterized by high levels of transparency, trust, and a strong commitment to delivering results.

I've worked with many organizations to help them shift their culture from previously lacking accountability and ownership to now thriving on individual responsibility. It's not a matter of just flipping a switch or pushing a button. Creating a culture of accountability takes buy-in and dedication from employees at all levels. I like to use the analogy of turning a big 747 airplane. The passengers on the airplane represent the people who are going to work day in and day out. You may not even realize that you're changing directions because it can be subtle and take some time. As an individual, you can have a significant impact on your organization's culture regardless of where you fall on an organizational chart. Your actions and behaviors are able to have ripple effects across an organization, regardless of its size.

Learning the Hard Way

I was promoted to the rank of sergeant between my deployment to Iraq and my first one to Afghanistan. We were stationed in Italy at the time and had been up in Germany conducting live-fire training and field exercises. The training rotations up to Germany were always difficult because we spent a lot of time out in the field, and you never knew what you would get weather-wise. And there was always a lot of mud.

By the time we got back to Italy, my buddies and I wanted to go out and celebrate my promotion. I was living in an apartment off the Army base in the city of Vicenza. We did all the right things: we put a plan together, we had a designated driver, and it was going to be awesome. Later on that night into the early morning I was pretty inebriated in the front passenger seat and I woke up to flashing lights. It was the Italian carabinieri—the Italian military police who also have civilian policing responsibilities. It was a random checkpoint. But I wasn't worried because we had our designated driver. It turned out that our designated driver did not have an Italian driver's license. I was surprised by this because part of every soldier's in-processing once they arrive in Italy is to go through a driving program to get an Italian license.

We were detained by the carabinieri, who called the US military police, who came and picked us up and brought us back to base. In turn, they called our commander and first sergeant in the very early morning, saying they had some knuckleheads here who had to be picked up. My section chief was the one who actually came to get me and lead me back to our headquarters area, where our commander and first sergeant were waiting. I was so nervous I felt like I was going to throw up—trust me, it wasn't because of the alcohol. The look of disappointment on their faces made me want to crawl under a rock and never be seen again.

I had an exceptional record in my career up until that point. We were not facing any legal trouble, but our commander had a difficult decision to make on our punishment. In the Army, nonjudicial punishment is called an Article 15 and there are three levels: a summary level, a company level, and a field-grade level. I was recommended for a field grade Article 15, the most severe level you can get. I had to move out of the apartment that I was living in and back into the Army barracks on base. I was restricted to base for 45 days straight, and I had 45 days of extra duty, which meant I was working from 5 a.m. until midnight for 45 days straight, and this was all happening over Christmas and New Year's 2004. They also took away a half-month's pay for two months. Normally with a field grade Article 15, they would take away your rank, demote you, and bust you down. But my commander—the one who just a few weeks prior had promoted me to sergeant, the one who recommended this level of punishment for me—actually went to his commander and fought for me to keep my rank, which is virtually unheard of. I've never seen it happen in any other circumstance. But I was fortunate to keep my rank.

Yet I was still in disbelief. My initial reaction was to feel like I was getting punished very harshly. I wasn't the one driving the car. It wasn't my fault that he didn't have an Italian license, right? But my initial reaction was wrong. That's not accountability, and that's not leadership. First of all, it was my car he was driving. I should have ensured he was a lawful driver. Second, when you are in a position of authority, you are also expected to be a leader. And I did not demonstrate good leadership judgment. Do you remember Jon Post, my platoon leader I told you about in

Chapter 6? He sat me down and we had one of those conversations where he tells you the 12 different ways you suck at life, but you leave the conversation ready to take on the world.

Forward-Looking Accountability

In one of our discussions, platoon leader Jon Post shared with me the idea of forward-looking accountability. Traditional notions of accountability are focused on the rear-view mirror. Someone does something wrong, we point the finger at them, and they get punished. That's basically how our judicial system works. But there are limits to the effectiveness of looking backward.

You can take things further with forward-looking accountability, which is a two-pronged approach. First, it's not about pointing the finger at someone else; it's about pointing the thumb at yourself. You look inside and see what your role was in the situation, develop ideas on how to prevent it from happening, and take action. Second, approach situations with the mindset of a crash investigator. Your number one goal should be to figure out exactly what happened, immediately take steps to prevent it from happening again, and communicate that with everyone who needs to know.

What might this look like in your organization? The idea is to embody a proactive and future-focused approach to organizational responsibility. Rather than concentrating solely on past performance or holding individuals accountable for past actions, this approach prioritizes planning, goal-setting, and continuous improvement to secure positive outcomes in the future. This approach is especially important to industries and organizations where adaptability and innovation are crucial.

This doesn't mean that people don't get in trouble for their actions, but it does mean that the blame game is not the number one focus. When you create a culture around forward-looking accountability, you help take down barriers that prevent people from having a growth mindset and allow them opportunities to think outside the box and develop solutions.

There is no official process to creating forward-looking accountability, but there are five key elements that need to be present if you want this to take hold across your culture:

1. **Strategic planning:** Organizations with a strong culture of forward-looking accountability actively engage in strategic planning. This involves setting long-term goals, identifying key priorities, and outlining strategies to achieve success.

2. **Continuous improvement:** The focus is on continuous learning and improvement. Rather than dwelling solely on past mistakes, the organization encourages feedback, learning from experiences, and making adjustments for better future outcomes.

3. **Adaptability:** Forward-looking accountability acknowledges the need for adaptability in the face of changing circumstances. It encourages cognitive flexibility and innovation to address evolving challenges and opportunities.

4. **Risk management:** The approach includes assessing and managing risks to prevent potential issues. Organizations should actively identify potential challenges and take steps to mitigate them before they impact performance.

5. **Feedback and development:** Regular feedback is provided to individuals and teams to help them understand their performance and identify areas for improvement. Development plans are created to support ongoing learning and skill enhancement.

Taking Accountability in the Heat
of the Moment

In Chapter 5, I mentioned how the attack on June 8, 2005, served as the unofficial start to the fighting season for us during our first deployment to Afghanistan. Things really ramped up that summer as we faced daily indirect fire attacks and participated in several large battles that saw between 50 and 100 enemy fighters each time. We were shooting our howitzers every day—whether it was returning fire on the indirect fire, supporting ground troops, or conducting harassment and interdiction fire—but there were a few large battles that really stood out and were actually captured via a high-tech camera that we had on a tall tower at our forward operating base (FOB).

That camera was manned 24/7 by soldiers and had great infrared and night vision capabilities, plus it could see for miles into the distance. The enemy liked to concentrate many of their attacks on the border control checkpoint that was about three miles down the road from the FOB. That checkpoint was manned by Afghan National Army soldiers. The surveillance guys we had were top notch and we were actually able to conduct fire missions with our howitzer cannons on the enemy via the camera alone. It was some pretty cutting-edge stuff at the time. And of course, all this was led by the great platoon leader Jon Post.

On one particular night, our surveillance guys caught a large cluster of about 100 enemy fighters streaming down the mountain that separated Afghanistan and Pakistan. We knew that they would cross the border, conduct their attacks, and then seek refuge back across the border again. This time we were on top of them before they even initiated their attack at the border control point. We started lobbing our rounds down range so fast that I think the enemy must have thought we had planted a tracker on them. At this time, I was the acting chief for our gun team, which meant it was my responsibility to shoot our rounds on target as efficiently and precisely as we could. This meant I had to verify the ammunition, the fuse, the powder charge, and the target data. The gunner could not fire the howitzer until I gave the command to fire.

As we fired our rounds, the enemy continued their attack on the border control checkpoint. During these types of missions, it took all-hands-on-deck running ammunition back and forth and digging into our storage bunker to bring out more. It was semi-organized chaos, with the thick smell of gunpowder and smoke hanging in the air, interrupted by the violent boom of the howitzer cannon firing.

Each fire mission came via radio to our ammunition team chief (ATC), who relayed all the information to me and the gunner. The other gun team was firing as well and received a fire mission for an illumination round. This requires them to shoot the mission at a high angle—basically the cannon tube is elevated more. As we continued to fire, I briefly heard a new mission come to our gun that said "special instructions, high angle." My immediate thought was that we were going to be firing an illumination round as well. As my gunner raised the tube, our platoon gunnery sergeant brought me an illumination round. He was always good about pitching in during situations like this. I verified the charge and fuse and gave the command to load. After the gun was set, I verified his data and sight picture and gave the command to fire. After we fired, a quiet stillness seemed to come over our gun pit.

"Burst on two," my ATC relayed over the radio to the fire direction center (FDC) as the illumination round lit up the night sky.

"Say again, over," replied the FDC.

"We've got burst on two," said my ATC.

"That was supposed to be an HE round, number two," said the FDC.

Apparently, we weren't supposed to be shooting an illumination round. Our round was supposed to be a high-explosive (HE) round with a variable timed fuse. It was a high-angle mission with that type of fuse because the enemy was seeking cover and the point detonation fuses were not as effective. No friendlies were hurt, and if anything, it probably scared the daylights out of the enemy as the illumination round burst right over their heads, as opposed to high up in the sky. I didn't have much time to dwell on this as the fight continued.

Once things had settled down, I looked around at the mess we had on our hands: empty ammunition boxes, power bags, and tired soldiers lying on the ground. Our platoon leader, Jon Post, came down to our gun pit and we talked about what had transpired with shooting the wrong round. Initially, my emotional reaction was wanting to point the finger at my ATC because he was the one listening to the radio, relaying information to me, and was supposed to verify each round that was brought to me. Then I wanted to point the finger at our platoon gunnery sergeant, a guy who outranked me and the one who had brought the round to me. Shouldn't he have brought me the correct round? Despite failures at different levels, I knew that I had to embrace a forward-looking accountability mindset. I could not point the finger at other soldiers for something that was ultimately my responsibility.

I also knew I had to be proactive and develop solutions to prevent that from happening again. I had a discussion with our entire gun team on what transpired and the steps we would implement, which included me standing closer to the radio so I could hear all the fire mission details. I also had a discussion with the FDC and we developed a plan where they would communicate with us if there were any unique circumstances, such as firing an HE round with a variable timed fuse at a high angle, compared to us consistently firing them at a lower angle with a point detonation fuse. Again, I reiterated my responsibility in this matter, but I appreciated everyone's willingness to help me develop solutions, so that mistake wouldn't happen again. That mindset was going to be tested again on my next deployment to Afghanistan.

Think about how this relates to the principles we've discussed so far. I used the two-pronged approach to look at my role in what happened and to consider how we could prevent repeating the mistake in the future. I also incorporated the five key elements of forward-looking accountability: I got feedback from the team, and we strategically planned to adapt and manage risks as part of our continuous improvement as a team.

As I said earlier in the book, most people won't experience a rocket getting shot at them or the challenge of shooting the wrong artillery round. Even so, sometimes you'll need to quickly take accountability in the heat of the moment, while other times you'll be able to put a little more time and thought into it. Let's take a look at what forward-looking accountability might look like for you.

Guiding Principles of Accountability

Imagine that you're a project manager responsible for a custom new product launch for your client. You're overseeing several different teams who are each working on tight deadlines to meet the client's delivery date. One of the teams falls behind schedule, and as the deadline approaches it becomes clear that this team will not be able to reach their milestones. As the project manager in this hypothetical situation, you should look for some telltale signs of a lack of accountability that might have led to this problem.

Here are some challenges I have found to be very common when different teams are working together toward one goal, yet are operating very independently of each other:

- **No updates:** The team fails to proactively communicate the challenges they are facing to the other teams or project managers. There's a lack of transparency regarding the project's status.

- **Lack of planning:** Despite falling behind, the team doesn't present a clear plan to address the delays. There's no initiative to reallocate resources, seek assistance, or make necessary adjustments to get back on track.

- **Pointing the finger:** When questioned about the delays, team members start blaming external factors, such as unforeseen technical issues or lack of support from other teams, without taking ownership of their role in the setback.

- **Unrealistic expectations:** There's a disconnect between the team's progress reports and the actual state of the project. Unrealistic expectations are set, and the team fails to deliver on promises made during previous status updates.

In a hypothetical situation like this, there are always numerous variables that can come in to play, just like in real life. But the good news is that there are practical things we can do as leaders to better help create a culture of accountability. Here are some guiding principles I've found helpful. Please note, this is not a step-by-step model you must follow in sequential order. I could give you great examples that fit neatly into a template, but we all know the real world rarely works like that. The key is that we recognize the variables that exist and remain proactive and committed to these guiding principles to create a culture of accountability.

- **Clear Communication:**
  - Ensure that expectations and goals are communicated clearly to every team member.
  - Encourage open communication channels to address questions and concerns—be approachable.
- **Define Expectations and Goals:**
  - Clearly articulate the organization's mission, vision, and values.
  - Establish specific, measurable, achievable, relevant, and time-bound (SMART) goals for teams and individuals.
- **Create Individual Development Plans:**
  - Collaborate with employees in creating individual development plans that align with the organization's objectives.
  - Clearly outline expectations for skill enhancement, performance advancement, and career progression.
- **Provide Training and Development:**
  - Offer training programs to enhance employees' skills and knowledge.
  - Invest in leadership development to empower managers to lead by example.

- **Promote Ownership:**
  - Encourage employees to take ownership of their work and responsibilities.
  - Celebrate successes and acknowledge accountability in the face of challenges.

- **Encourage Initiative and Innovation:**
  - Reward and recognize employees who take the initiative and contribute innovative ideas.
  - Create an environment where employees feel empowered to suggest improvements and take calculated risks.

- **Provide Regular Feedback:**
  - Conduct regular feedback sessions to discuss performance, identify areas for improvement, and recognize achievements.
  - Ensure that feedback is constructive and focuses on continuous improvement.

- **Address Issues Promptly:**
  - Act swiftly to address performance issues or violations of organizational policies.
  - Provide support and resources to help employees overcome challenges.

- **Lead by Example:**
  - Leadership sets the tone for accountability. Leaders should demonstrate accountability in their actions and decisions.
  - Hold leaders accountable for their responsibilities and behaviors.

- **Celebrate Success and Learn from Failure:**
  - Celebrate achievements and milestones to reinforce a culture of success.
  - View failures as opportunities for learning and improvement, encouraging a resilient and accountable mindset.

Creating a culture of accountability is a continual endeavor that demands dedication and sustained contributions from all levels of an organization. Promoting ownership, defining expectations, and offering essential support and resources contribute to creating an environment where accountability flourishes.

Rolling with a Culture of Accountability

In the summer of 2007, I found myself up at Observation Post (OP) Warheit in the Nuristan Province in the mountains of northeast Afghanistan. Our platoon was tasked with manning this small OP and guarding Combat Outpost (COP) Keating, which was set in a notoriously dangerous and illogical location several thousand meters below the OP in a valley with a raging river running next to it.

I was in charge of one of the two squads in our platoon. We were supposed to do two-week rotations up to the OP. It had very austere conditions with no running water, no hot chow, and no showers. My squad ended up being there for 40 days straight. But we didn't mind. There were 14 soldiers up there and I was the highest-ranking person, but again, that is just a position of authority. My actions and behaviors are what made me a leader, not my title.

Our mission was twofold: we served overwatch over the valley below, and we served as a retransmission station so the two bases on each side of the mountain could still communicate via radio as we had a large antenna on top of the mountain. With no real authority figures up there other than myself, it almost felt like many of the pictures I remember seeing of soldiers in Vietnam, cutting off the sleeves of our shirts, growing our hair out, not shaving. We thought we were pretty cool.

We had a small 5k generator that kept our batteries charged and the antenna powered up. And every once in a while, a Chinook helicopter would fly in with a 500-gallon fuel blivit sling loaded underneath. It basically looked like a big tractor tire made out of hard, galvanized rubber that was literally hanging from a rope under the helicopter as it flew.

Because we were literally on a mountain, there was no place for the helicopter to land. We had a small, flat, but not level piece of ground that the helicopter would hover over and gently set the fuel blivit down. My soldiers would put a rock in front of the blivit so it wouldn't roll away, and then the helicopter would unhook the rope and fly away. We'd trained for it many times, we'd done it here many times, and this day was supposed to be no different.

I was standing up at the tactical operations center, which is a fancy Army word for our tent with the radio. We all took shifts watching the radio, and this happened to be my turn. Did I have to take a radio shift? Nope. But I learned from great leaders before me that we need to lead from the front and it was a small opportunity to give my guys a little bit of a break.

I was standing outside the tent watching as the helicopter came in, hovered overhead, and gently set down the fuel blivit. My soldier placed a rock in front it, and the helicopter unhooked and flew away. Just as my soldiers were about to hook the fuel blivit up to a six-wheeled gator vehicle to inch it back up the rest of the mountain, my soldier pulled the rock out from it, and it started to slowly roll down the landing zone.

My soldiers stared in shock because they knew there wasn't anything they could do. I was yelling every four-letter word

I knew except "stop." And there was no stopping it. It picked up steam and went over the side of the mountain, bursting open about a thousand meters down the side. And now I was going to have to hop on the radio and let them know that we needed them to fly back through that dangerous valley—risking their lives again—where the enemy liked to shoot RPGs and machine guns at them, because we had messed up.

If that had happened early in my career, I would have hopped on that radio and said, "Well, Mitchell did it, he pulled out the rock, it was his fault." But that's not leadership and that's not accountability. Although I failed to prevent that incident from happening, I was still able to exercise some aspects of forward-looking accountability by taking ownership of the situation and looking at my role. Before the fuel delivery, I could have just held a little pre-mission huddle with my soldiers, just to remind them what everyone's task was—but I hadn't done that. I also could have made another soldier take my radio shift, which I had the authority to do, so I could have been down there supervising the operation—but I hadn't done that. So I got on the radio and let them know that I had lost the fuel, and it was my fault.

Later that afternoon, we conducted our standard After Action Review (AAR). An AAR is debriefing process that takes place after a mission, training exercise, or operation. Its purpose is to analyze what happened, why it happened, and how to improve future performance. During an AAR, soldiers discuss and evaluate the actions taken, the effectiveness of the plan, and any issues or challenges encountered. The goal is to identify lessons learned, successes, and areas for improvement. What I remember most about this was how all of my soldiers stood up and identified something they could have done differently to prevent the situation from happening. None of them got up and pointed the finger at the guy who pulled the rock out. They all demonstrated what forward-looking accountability is. It felt like one of those proud parent moments where you are like, "Yes! You understand it!"

We've covered a lot of ground in this chapter discussing how to create a culture of accountability. It can't be done overnight but it can be done through the consistent actions that you demonstrate on a daily basis. Remember, it's a lot easier to be accountable when things are going right, but the true test of leadership is being accountable when things go wrong.

Your Challenge

Just like your challenge at the end of Chapter 7 with the vision board workshop, I challenge you to hold an accountability building workshop. This will help you reinforce the importance of accountability and empower your team to hold each other accountable. It is designed to be interactive and practical.

Here is what to do:

1. **Introduction (10 minutes):** Start the workshop by discussing the importance of accountability within the team. Emphasize how accountability contributes to the team's success and overall effectiveness.

2. **Group Discussion (15 minutes):** Facilitate a discussion about what accountability means to the team members. Encourage them to share their thoughts, experiences, and expectations regarding accountability. If you think people might have difficulty talking about this, give them a prompt

question prior to the workshop, such as "Find any image you want that speaks to you on what accountability looks like in your role." Images are great kick starters to meaningful conversations.

3. **Identify Key Responsibilities (15 minutes)**: Use a whiteboard or flip chart to list key responsibilities and tasks within the team. Ask team members to contribute and ensure that all major responsibilities are covered.

4. **Define Expectations (20 minutes)**: Break down each responsibility into specific tasks and discuss the expectations for each task. Make sure that the expectations are clear, measurable, and align with the team's goals.

5. **Accountability Partnerships (15 minutes)**: Pair team members to be accountability partners. Explain the concept and ask each pair to discuss how they can support and hold each other accountable for their respective tasks.

6. **Action Planning (15 minutes)**: Ask each team member to create a personal action plan for enhancing their accountability. What specific steps will they take to ensure they meet their responsibilities, and how will they support their accountability partners?

7. **Group Commitment (10 minutes)**: Conclude the workshop by having each team member share one commitment they are making to enhance accountability within the team. Encourage a collective commitment to fostering a culture of accountability.

8. **Follow-up (Ongoing)**: Schedule regular follow-up sessions to discuss progress, address challenges, and celebrate successes related to accountability. This ensures that accountability remains a focus within the team.

10

Building a Positive Workplace Culture

CHAPTER

Building a Positive
Workplace Culture

A positive workplace culture is essential for the well-being and overall success of an organization. I've experienced both sides of the coin when it comes to the culture of an organization, positive ones and negative ones, and I would imagine you have as well. Organizations that have a positive culture are defined by an atmosphere that fosters employee well-being, collaboration, and a shared sense of purpose. This contributes to high morale, job satisfaction, and overall organizational success.

The word "culture" can sometimes be seen as a part of an organization that is out of our control as individuals. But it doesn't matter what our position or title is—we can all have an impact. Just as one bad apple can spoil a bunch, I honestly believe that one person has the ability to have an outsized positive impact on an organization's culture by demonstrating the right behaviors on a consistent basis and influencing others to do the same.

In this chapter, we're going to explore not only the benefits of a positive workplace culture and what it actually looks like, but also some very practical tips that you as an individual can start using today. We'll take a look at some real-world examples of organizational cultures—some of which have succeeded better than others.

Why a Positive Workplace Culture Matters

When we work for an organization that has a negative culture, it takes a toll on us not only as employees but also as people. It's difficult to separate our work and personal lives these days, and a bad day at work can carry over to our life at home. The pervasive stress, toxicity, and discontentment experienced at work can easily follow us home and strain our connections with family and friends. Dissatisfaction with our professional environment has the potential to diminish our sense of purpose and self-esteem, influencing not only our job satisfaction but also our overall personal development. The amount of time and energy that we have invested in navigating a toxic work environment can hurt our opportunities for personal growth, self-care, and just enjoying life.

If you were nodding your head as you were reading that last paragraph, you've either experienced that type of culture or might be in one right now. It would be really easy for me to tell you that you should just go find another job if you're in that boat right now. But I know that's a lot easier said than done, plus I'm all about facing challenges head on and making a difference. Building a positive workplace culture is crucial for many reasons. Here are my top five reasons why it matters:

1. **Employee Satisfaction and Engagement:** A positive culture contributes to higher levels of employee satisfaction and engagement. When employees feel valued, supported, and fulfilled in their roles, they are more likely to be motivated, committed, and actively involved in their work.

2. **Retaining Talent:** It's no secret that the cost of hiring a new employee is exponentially higher than retaining one. It's a lot easier for organizations with a positive culture to retain top talent. Employees are more likely to stay with a company where they feel a sense of belonging, see opportunities for growth, and enjoy a positive work environment.

3. **Collaboration:** When we're working in positive environments, we're more likely to communicate openly, share ideas, and

work together toward common goals, leading to improved problem-solving and innovation. By contrast, in negative cultures most people are walking on eggshells—they keep their heads down for fear of rocking the boat.

4. **Customer Satisfaction:** I'm sure most of us have seen the unfortunate videos of unhappy customers making a scene in a restaurant or store. Happy and engaged employees are more likely to provide excellent customer service. The importance of a positive workplace culture on customer satisfaction, loyalty, and positive word-of-mouth about the company cannot be overstated.

5. **Increased Productivity:** Fostering a positive workplace culture results in increased productivity. When employees experience happiness and motivation, they tend to exhibit enhanced focus, creativity, and efficiency in their tasks. This positive mindset contributes significantly to the overall success of the organization.

The culture of our workplace impacts employee engagement, customer satisfaction, productivity, collaboration, and the ability to attract and retain top talent. As organizations recognize the importance of creating a positive work environment, they are better positioned to achieve long-term success and growth. It might seem like a no-brainer that having a positive workplace culture is good, yet it doesn't always happen.

When a Workplace Culture Has Problems

Pop quiz: what healthcare technology startup was once valued at $10 billion but no longer exists due to significant ethical and legal challenges? If you guessed Theranos, you are correct. Theranos was a startup on a meteoric rise that promised to revolutionize the at-home healthcare industry with just a prick of the finger and a drop of blood. The organization raised billions of dollars all on an idea led by their founder, Elizabeth Holmes.

Initially, Theranos garnered acclaim for its ambitious vision and groundbreaking approach to healthcare, with Holmes often depicted as a charismatic and visionary leader. The company successfully attracted top talent from esteemed institutions, drawing many employees who were inspired by the mission to make healthcare more accessible and convenient. However, subsequent investigations uncovered significant problems with the company's technology and practices. Ultimately, it was discovered that Theranos hadn't been clearly and accurately transparent with investors, patients, and the public regarding the capabilities of its technology. Consequently, both Holmes and another executive were sentenced to prison for their respective roles in the scandal.

Accounts of the Theranos workplace culture indicated a prevalence of secrecy and a climate of fear for individuals questioning the company's practices. Employees were purportedly discouraged from sharing information about their work with colleagues, and there were claims of a tightly regulated and hierarchical environment. The demanding expectations to achieve ambitious goals and meet deadlines inevitably contributed to a high-stress atmosphere.

When a Workplace Culture Works Well

The Container Store is an example of a company that is often praised for its positive workplace culture. The Container Store is a retail company specializing in storage and organization solutions. The company's commitment to creating a positive workplace culture has contributed to its reputation as a great place to work—often ranking in the top of the best places to work lists. What makes it so special? Here are some of the key features:

- **Values-driven culture:** Most organizations have a list of company values on their website or hanging on the wall in their office. But it's one thing to exist on a list and it's a completely different thing to actually embody and live the values—which the Container Store is known for. They have a strong values-driven culture, and their core values are deeply embedded in the company's operations. These values include communication, leadership, and a commitment to both employees and customers.

- **Employee empowerment:** The Container Store places a strong emphasis on employee empowerment. In Chapter 7 we talked about the power of autonomy and how it can motivate others, and the Container Store is known for empowering employees to make decisions and contribute to the success of the company.

- **Recognition and appreciation:** The Container Store values and recognizes the contributions of its employees. There are programs in place to acknowledge and reward outstanding performance, fostering a culture of appreciation. (I'm going to share some of my personal experiences around recognition later in the chapter.)

- **Focus on training and development:** The company invests in the training and development of its employees. There are extensive training programs to ensure that employees are well equipped to assist customers and excel in their roles.

- **Employee benefits and well-being:** The company provides a range of benefits to support the well-being of its employees. This includes health and wellness programs, as well as initiatives to promote work-life balance.

Organizations like the Container Store are out there, and they come in all shapes and sizes across every industry.

People often view challenges such as building a positive workplace culture from a deficit mindset, meaning they only focus on the negative. I think it is just as important to identify the strengths of a culture and learn how to continually leverage those as well. The Container Store might enjoy a positive workplace culture, but that doesn't mean they can't make it even better. The same is true for all workplace cultures.

How to Make a Difference

As leaders, we may not transform our entire organization overnight, but our actions, behaviors, and values can influence the mindset and behaviors of our colleagues, gradually contributing to the evolution of the organization's culture. Remember, we're not turning a fighter jet, we're turning a 747 commercial jet, and it takes time. Here are 10 things that you can do to start that turn:

1. **Create a Clear Mission and Vision:** Clearly articulate the organization's mission and vision. A well-defined purpose provides team members with a sense of direction and helps them understand the broader impact of their work.

2. **Promote Open Communication:** Establish open lines of communication at all levels of the organization. Encourage

regular feedback, both upward and downward, to ensure that employees feel heard and valued. Foster an environment where diverse perspectives are welcomed.

3. **Promote Autonomy:** Empower employees to make decisions and contribute to the organization's success. Providing autonomy and recognizing employees' abilities to take ownership of their work fosters a sense of responsibility and commitment. Ensure you are providing your people with all the resources they need to be successful.

4. **Promote Work-Life Balance:** We've all known the importance of work-life balance and we've seen organizations talk about it for years. Now it's time to start doing more to actually achieve it. Encourage reasonable working hours, flexibility, and time-off policies that support employees in achieving a healthy balance between their professional and personal lives.

5. **Establish a Recognition Culture:** Create a culture of appreciation and recognition. Regularly acknowledge and celebrate individual and team achievements. Recognition can take various forms, including verbal praise, awards, or peer-to-peer recognition programs.

6. **Encourage Inclusivity and Diversity:** Foster an inclusive workplace that values diversity. Embrace diverse perspectives, backgrounds, and experiences. Implement inclusive policies and practices to create a sense of belonging for all employees.

7. **Promote Wellness Programs:** Implement wellness programs that support employees' physical and mental well-being. These programs can include fitness initiatives, mental health resources, and activities that promote a healthy lifestyle. A lot of great organizations will sponsor employees who participate in fitness events such as marathons, 5ks, and the like.

8. **Provide Opportunities for Social Interaction:** Facilitate social interactions among employees through events, team outings, or casual gatherings. Positive relationships outside of work tasks contribute to a supportive and enjoyable workplace. Remember, you don't need to be best friends, but the research is clear: the more we know each other, the higher performing our teams and organizations are.

9. **Address Conflict Effectively:** Develop strategies for addressing conflicts in a constructive manner. Establishing open channels for conflict resolution and providing training on effective communication can help prevent and resolve issues promptly.

10. **Flexibility and Adaptability:** Cultivate a culture of flexibility and adaptability to respond to changing circumstances. Employees who feel supported in navigating change are more likely to contribute positively to the organization's success.

Like everything we've been discussing in this book, consistency is key when implementing these strategies. A positive work culture is built over time through intentional efforts and a commitment to creating an environment where employees feel valued, supported, and motivated.

The Power of Respect and Recognition

I've been fortunate to be awarded some medals during my time in the Army, including the Bronze Star Medal, the Purple Heart Medal, and three Army Commendation Medals. There was a lot of formality when each of those medals were pinned on my uniform. The military loves pomp and circumstance. I am proud of my service and of having earned those awards. However, it surprises many people when I tell them that I keep those in a storage locker tucked away under the steps at home. But what I do keep on my desk is my rack of coins that I was presented during my time in the military.

These coins are commonly known as Challenge Coins or Coins of Excellence. Many commanders and sergeant majors have their own unique coin design, often emblazed with their unit motto and/or insignia. There are some really creative ones out there. These coins are often presented to a service member for something that they've done. The vast majority of my coins were given to me during my deployments to Iraq and Afghanistan.

For example, the commanding general would come and visit us and he'd ask the platoon leader to pick a soldier or two who had really busted their butt, and he would present them with a coin in front of the entire platoon. I've always been very proud of my coin collection because I feel like it is an accurate representation of the effort I put forward. I can even recall where and why the majority of coins were given. I'll never forget the first one.

In the summer of 2003, I was a young solider in Iraq and our platoon was tasked with operating out of a safehouse in the town of Taza, which was home to an estimated 27,000 Iraqis. Our platoon consisted of two squads and our mission included standard infantry patrols along with some forming cordons and conducting searches. The fall of the Iraqi government in the spring of 2003 had left a void that caused a lot of challenges for local municipal governments, and part of our mission was to get them up and running again. Since we were very limited on manpower, every noncommissioned officer in our platoon was assigned responsibility for a department within the city. This included acting as a liaison with the Iraqi civilians and navigating the difficult grant program to get money flowing into the communities.

At this time, I had the rank of specialist, which is one rank below a noncommissioned officer. But due to our shortage, our commander assigned me to the parks and recreation department of the city of Taza. I chuckle at that now because I think he knew that was where I could do the least amount of damage. At the time I took it very seriously. I worked hard and put together a plan to get a soccer field created for local youth. This included finding and acquiring land, putting together a budget, getting bids, and completing a mountain of paperwork required by the Provincial Reconstruction Teams—the approving authority for funding.

Although it was not necessary, I put together a snazzy PowerPoint presentation to lay out all the information. That was the first time I ever used PowerPoint and it took some time to learn. Heck, it was the first time I've done any of that type of work. We still conducted all of our patrols while also working on the other assignments. I was definitely motivated by the autonomy that I was provided and the purpose-driven nature of the work.

A few weeks later, the brigade executive officer, Lieutenant Colonel Randy George, made a visit out to our safehouse. A fun fact about Randy George: he was eventually promoted to the rank of four-star general and held the highest position in the Army as the chief of staff of the Army. He presented me with the Brigade Coin for the work I had done. I felt like he handed me a thousand dollars. I was and still am very proud of that coin; I felt like it really recognized my contributions. I'm not saying the other shiny medals I've been awarded don't also recognize it, but many of those are for the totality of work—much like a 10-, 20-, 30-year award some people receive for their service in an organization. The recognition provided to me, and other soldiers, helped serve as a building block in fostering a positive workplace culture.

I often ask people what type of recognition programs their organizations have. It's pretty sad when someone tells me all about this terrific program but another person in the same room who has been with the company for five years says they've never heard of it. Many organizations have invested in these great programs and it's incumbent upon leaders to use them effectively. It's important to recognize the work and effort our people put forward.

You may work for an organization that doesn't have one of these programs. If so, guess what? That's no excuse. There are still things you can do to recognize the efforts of your people. Here are 10 awesome ideas that cost little to no money:

1. **Employee of the Month/Quarter/Year Awards:** Implement an employee recognition program with awards for outstanding performance. Highlight achievements, dedication, and positive contributions. One organization I worked for didn't have this, but it didn't stop a team lead from creating one for his team. There was no fancy plaque on the wall, but he got a professional wrestling-style belt—one you in can find the toy aisles—and at the end of every month would award it to one of his team members. It became a fun and engaging way for the team to stay connected and challenged.

2. **Personalized Thank-You Notes or Phone Calls:** Write personalized thank-you notes expressing appreciation for specific contributions. Handwritten notes show a personal touch and make employees feel valued. Another great idea is to ask a senior member of the organization to call an employee and let them know they appreciate their efforts. I've seen this work really well when CEOs call front-line employees to recognize their hard work.

3. **Peer-to-Peer Recognition:** Encourage a culture of peer recognition where colleagues can nominate each other for outstanding efforts. This fosters a sense of camaraderie and teamwork. Some organizations have formal programs in place where colleagues can do this. If yours doesn't have one yet, go out there and start it.

4. **Public Acknowledgment:** Recognize employees publicly during team meetings, company-wide announcements, or in newsletters. Share their achievements with the entire organization. Praise in public, discipline in private.

5. **Flexible Work Arrangements:** Offer flexible work arrangements, such as remote workdays or flexible hours, as a way of acknowledging and accommodating employees' needs. One of the biggest benefits from employers that job candidates are looking for is flexibility.

6. **Celebratory Lunch or Dinner:** Arrange a team lunch or dinner to celebrate accomplishments or milestones. This creates a relaxed and enjoyable atmosphere for acknowledging efforts. I encourage you to do this over normal working hours—don't make people take their own unpaid time to do this.

7. **Gift Cards or Vouchers:** Gift cards or vouchers for popular stores, restaurants, or experiences are versatile and can be

tailored to individual preferences. Gift cards are easy—they are portable. I know many great leaders who always have a couple on hand at all times when walking the floor or visiting their people.

8. **Company Swag:** Provide branded company merchandise such as T-shirts, mugs, or notebooks as a token of appreciation. Employees can proudly use or wear these items. You may be tempted to blow this off and say you don't need another company shirt. However, I've seen how this stuff can be worth its weight in gold for some employees. The bottom line is that you need to know what your people like.

9. **Team Building Activities:** Organize team-building activities or outings as a way of expressing gratitude and fostering team spirit. And just like a celebratory meal, do it during normal work hours.

10. **Time Off or Extended Weekends:** The three-day or four-day weekend is something that was done in the military and always greatly appreciated. Offer additional days off or extended weekends as a gesture of appreciation for a job well done. Of course, make sure you pay them, too.

When you implement these ideas, try to really understand how they fit into your existing culture. If your organization pays low wages for long hours and upper management lives in mansions with in-ground swimming pools and comes to work in luxury sports cars, a paper or virtual gold star for an employee of the month might not carry much value on its own. But if it is paired with a gift card or an extra day off with pay, that can make all the difference. On the other side of the coin, if your people are passionately invested in your organization, specially designed T-shirts commemorating their unique accomplishment this year might be worth more to them than a paid day off. It's important to reward your people with what matters to them.

Recognition is a powerful tool for shaping organizational culture by promoting positive behaviors, fostering engagement, and creating a workplace where individuals feel valued and motivated. It contributes to a culture that aligns with the organization's values and promotes overall success.

The journey of building a positive workplace culture is a dynamic and ongoing process that requires commitment, adaptability, and a shared vision among organizational members, and it can start with you. The influence of a positive workplace culture extends far beyond the physical workspace; it can also be seen in employee attitudes, engagement levels, and the collective sense of purpose that propels the organization forward. When you're working toward building a positive workplace culture, you help lay the foundation for a resilient, innovative, and collaborative workplace where individuals find fulfillment in their roles, and the organization as a whole reaps the rewards of enhanced productivity and sustained success.

Your Challenge

I'm big on recognition and the value it brings to an organization. I've facilitated challenges called the Recognition Wall across a variety of organizations and industries. It's not only a great way to highlight individual achievement but also to create positivity around the organization's accomplishments. Here is what you need to do:

1. **Introduction:** Explain the purpose of the Recognition Wall activity: to publicly acknowledge and appreciate the efforts

and achievements of individual employees within the team. Provide a designated wall or bulletin board along with sticky notes, markers, tacks, and so on.

2. **Recognition Categories:** Define specific recognition categories based on the team's goals, values, or ongoing projects. For example, categories could include "Innovation and Creativity," "Team Player Award," or "Customer Service Excellence." The more creative, the better.

3. **Team Discussion:** Facilitate a discussion with the team to determine the criteria for each recognition category. Encourage input from all team members to ensure a collaborative approach.

4. **Nomination Process:** Establish a process for nominating colleagues for recognition. This could involve team members submitting anonymous nominations or openly acknowledging each other's achievements.

5. **Display on Recognition Wall:** Invite team members to affix their recognition cards to the Recognition Wall. Arrange the cards under the appropriate categories.

6. **Monthly Recognition Ceremony:** Schedule a monthly recognition ceremony or team meeting to formally announce and celebrate the individuals recognized on the wall. Share the achievements and express gratitude for the positive impact on the team.

7. **Keep It Fresh:** Regularly rotate the recognition cards on the wall to ensure that different team members receive acknowledgment. Update the categories as needed to align with changing priorities and goals.

8. **Seek Feedback:** Encourage team members to provide feedback on the Recognition Wall. Ask for suggestions on how to enhance the recognition process and make it more meaningful for everyone.

11

Engaging and Empowering Others to Lead Cultural Change

Driving cultural change is a deliberate effort to reshape the way people think, act, and interact within a group. This could be a group of 10 people on your team at work or a companywide cultural shift of over 1,000 people. The need for change is often driven by a recognition that the existing culture may no longer be conducive to the organization's goals, or that changes are needed to adapt to evolving external factors.

In the last two chapters, we've talked about creating a culture of accountability and building a positive workplace culture. In this chapter, we're going to bring those ideas together and examine how we can engage and empower others to help us lead cultural change in our organizations. I'll share some experiences of mine that have shaped how I view cultural change and why I believe we all can impact our organizational culture in a meaningful way. We're also going to explore some examples of organizations that have engaged and empowered leaders to drive cultural change while also providing some practical takeaways aimed at helping you to do the same in your organization.

Engage and Empower

I'm a big fan of alliteration but it's important to understand the difference between engagement and empowerment. Both of these concepts are related—they each help create a positive and productive environment at work, but they focus on some very different aspects of the employee experience. A simplified way to think of it is that engagement refers to the emotional connection that employees have with their work, while empowerment involves providing autonomy, delegating authority, and equipping people with the resources necessary to make decisions. Here are some other key differences:

- **Performance Emphasis:**
  - **Engagement:** Frequently associated with heightened productivity, collaborative efforts, and an overall positive working environment
  - **Empowerment:** Often linked to improved decision-making, innovation, and a sense of ownership and accountability
- **Fundamental Connection:**
  - **Engagement:** Relates to the employees' commitment, motivation, and sense of belonging to the organization
  - **Empowerment:** Involves the extent of control, influence, and autonomy that employees possess in relation to their work and decision-making procedures
- **Focus of Attention:**
  - **Engagement:** Focuses on the emotional and psychological connection employees have with their work, team, and organization
  - **Empowerment:** Focuses on providing employees with the authority and autonomy to make decisions and take control of their work
- **Course of Influence:**
  - **Engagement:** Encompasses how organizational culture, leadership, and the work environment shape the mindset and commitment of employees
  - **Empowerment:** Involves the influence of the organization in providing opportunities, resources, and support for employees to take ownership of their roles

- **Time Perspective:**
  - **Engagement:** Reflects the ongoing commitment and motivation of employees over time
  - **Empowerment:** Relates to the immediate and ongoing actions and decisions employees are empowered to make

Engaged and empowered employees are likely to be more satisfied, motivated, and effective contributors to the organization's success. Organizations often seek to achieve high levels of both engagement and empowerment as part of a holistic approach to creating a positive and high-performing workplace, but we know that doesn't always happen. I experienced firsthand what happens when there is a disconnect among leadership when it comes to engagement and empowerment and the challenges it places on an organization.

Iron Fist

I was fortunate to spend the vast majority of my military career with the historic 173rd Airborne Brigade based out of Vicenza, Italy. Our brigade consisted of several smaller units within it. A lot of members of our unit had mixed feelings about our commander. I caught wind of this pretty early on when I heard the noncommissioned officers in my unit speak about him. I honestly hadn't been there long enough to really form an opinion so I tried to keep an open mind.

As our unit geared up to deploy to Iraq in March of 2003, rumors swirled about what our mission would entail. Our commander was pretty tight-lipped on what we would be doing, while other soldiers I knew had commanders who were very open and transparent about what the mission was, which better helped them prepare mentally for what they would face. In the absence of information, people tend to fill in the blanks themselves, often resulting in unnecessary confusion and turmoil.

On March 26, 2003, under the cover of darkness, elements of the 173rd Airborne Brigade parachuted into northern Iraq in the largest mass combat jump since the Vietnam War. I did not get to jump that night because the drop zone was thick with mud and would have buried our 105mm howitzer cannons on the heavy drop. We arrived the next night via a large C-17 airplane that landed on a small, bumpy airstrip nestled between snowcapped mountains in northern Iraq. When the sun began to rise the following morning, we saw green grass and lots of mud. Many of us joked that they flew us around for six hours and dropped us in Germany for a training exercise because this was not what we had envisioned Iraq looking like. I mean, where was all the sand?

Our brigade's mission was basically to be a distraction to the Iraqi military units in the north and prevent them from reinforcing other Iraqi units in the south, where the spearhead of the coalition mission was moving in from Kuwait. It was literally called Operation Northern Delay—as in delay these Iraqi troops. After about a week of remaining near the airfield we landed on, two of our gun sections were ordered to push south and told to be ready to conduct artillery raids against Iraqi troops. My section was one of them.

The commander of our unit was known to rule with an iron fist and micromanage his troops. He was the opposite of a guy like my former platoon leader Jon Post. On April 6, 2003, we conducted our first two-gun artillery raid against Iraqi targets. As we rolled into our firing location, the stillness of the night made it all feel so surreal as my mind wandered to the journey that I had been on to get to this point. From writing letters in the second grade to soldiers in Operation Desert Storm to enlisting in the Army right after 9/11, it kind of felt like a dream. I quickly snapped back to reality as I loaded the first round into our howitzer cannon and the loud boom shook the earth beneath my feet. Our two guns had fired the first rounds in combat for our storied brigade since the Vietnam War. We fired numerous rounds that night and the adrenaline was pumping through all of us.

While we were firing our rounds, our commander got out of his vehicle and grabbed a couple of the brass canisters from the rounds that we fired. This gave the impression that he was more concerned with collecting mementos than taking care of his troops and helping us do our jobs. That's not the ideal model of what to do as a leader. The culture that he created felt limiting and constraining to many of the officers and soldiers in our unit, leading to low morale and a strong desire to leave our unit.

Turning the Culture Around

After we had established a foothold in the northern Iraqi city of Kirkuk, we soon got a new commander, Captain J. Shay Howard. Captain Howard was a former enlisted soldier who became a commissioned officer. These types of officers are often referred to as mustang officers, and they bring a unique perspective from having been in the shoes of the enlisted people they are tasked with leading. I could tell right away that things were going to be very different with Captain Howard.

We conducted an abbreviated change of command ceremony on a grassy field at the airbase where our brigade was based. Immediately after the ceremony, Captain Howard sat down with many of us and spoke to us on a level that we did not have with our previous commander. He didn't talk about the work. He wanted to get to know us. He didn't come across as someone who thought he was better than us because he was the commander. And that spoke volumes to us about the type of person that he was and helped set the tone for his command.

One of the most important things that Captain Howard did was empower his lieutenants and sergeants to make decisions. He understood that we all had the boots-on-the-ground perspective as it related to our mission and the challenges. He did not create unnecessary meetings, reports, and red tape. You could tell that he had a high level of trust in his front-line leaders to do the right thing. He also understood the importance of leadership visibility as he made it a priority to spend time out with his troops. I remember him spending several nights with us in our safehouse in the city of Taza and the relaxed atmosphere he brought with him. He enjoyed getting to know each soldier personally and didn't hesitate to jump in and play cards with us.

Our missions changed several times over the following months, and with every change Captain Howard was upfront and transparent in his communication. One of these changes involved us dusting off our howitzer cannons—which had been packed away since the early start of the war—and heading to a small city to the west of Kirkuk that was becoming a hotbed of insurgent activity. Captain Howard provided our platoon with the mission and let our leadership create the plan to get us there and to put our guns into action. The two-lane highway to this location was littered with craters from past IED attacks. I have to say, driving in Iraq was always the scariest thing for me—there wasn't a lot we could do at the time to defend against IEDs, and our brigade was not issued armored vehicles like most of the other units were. In fact, our Humvees were known as the soft-skin type, so we actually removed the doors as they were not going to stop anything, and it made it easier to react to contact if necessary. We had no gun turrets on our Humvees and had to use ratchet straps on a piece of plywood to hold the machine gun in place while driving.

I'll never forget that day we drove out to our new home away from home. We immediately got our howitzer cannons set up and ready to fire. Step one complete. The next thing we did was start to dig what are known as ranger graves: small holes in the ground that we could dive into to give us a little bit of cover if we came under attack. And sure enough, we got attacked less than an hour after rolling in to position. My good friend Johnny Pineda and I still laugh to this day about that attack as we both dove into ranger graves next to each other and he said the expression on my face said it all—it looked like I had seen a ghost and all the blood had drained from my face. We needed to fortify the location as best as we could, and Captain Howard made sure we had every resource available to us.

Captain Howard was eventually promoted to Major Howard and was my commander at the beginning of my next deployment when I was wounded in Afghanistan. His leadership and ability to engage and empower all of us soldiers helped turn around the culture in our unit. I was honored to serve with him and am honored to call him a friend and someone I still stay in contact with.

Working Together

When it comes to changing culture, it always helps to have allies on your side who will support you and your mission. But they're not going to do it just because you tell them to. When we lead with our rank or title, we get the minimum amount of compliance, but when we lead through influence, we tap into that coveted trait known as discretionary effort. When you combine the strategies behind engagement and empowerment, you can create an environment where individuals feel engaged, empowered, and motivated to actively contribute to cultural change.

Remember that cultural change is an ongoing process, and maintaining momentum requires consistent effort and attention. Here are some strategies to help you in your mission:

- **Communication Is Key:**
  - Clearly communicate the reasons behind the cultural change. Help employees understand the benefits and the long-term vision.
  - Maintain open and transparent communication channels. Encourage questions and provide regular updates.
- **Involve Employees in the Process:**
  - Include employees in decision-making processes related to the cultural change. Seek their input on key decisions and let them be part of the solution.
  - Establish cross-functional teams to work on specific aspects of the cultural change.
- **Create a Shared Vision:**
  - Develop a shared vision for the desired culture. Ensure that employees feel connected to and inspired by this vision.

- Emphasize how each individual's role contributes to the overall success of the cultural transformation.
- **Leadership Alignment:**
  - Ensure that leaders at all levels are aligned with the cultural change. Leaders should embody the values and behaviors expected from employees.
  - Provide leadership training if necessary to equip leaders with the skills to lead through change.
- **Recognize and Celebrate Progress:**
  - Acknowledge and celebrate small wins along the way. This helps build momentum and keeps employees motivated.
  - Recognize individuals and teams for their contributions to the cultural change.
- **Provide Resources and Training:**
  - Equip employees with the tools and resources they need to adapt to the new culture.
  - Offer training programs that support the development of skills and behaviors aligned with the desired culture.
- **Feedback Mechanisms:**
  - Establish regular feedback mechanisms to gather insights from employees. Use surveys, focus groups, and other methods to understand their concerns and ideas.
  - Act on feedback promptly, demonstrating that their input is valued.
- **Lead by Example:**
  - Leadership should exemplify the desired cultural values. Employees are more likely to adopt the new culture if they see leaders actively practicing it.
  - Encourage leaders to share personal stories that illustrate the importance of the cultural change.

- **Foster a Supportive Environment:**
  - Create an environment that supports risk-taking and innovation. Encourage employees to experiment with new ways of working and reward creative problem-solving.
  - Provide support for employees who may be struggling to adapt to the changes.

- **Continuous Improvement:**
  - Cultures are dynamic, and ongoing assessment and adaptation are necessary. Regularly evaluate the effectiveness of the cultural change efforts and make adjustments as needed.

With those strategies in mind, take a look at the following hypothetical scenario and think about what you might do as the CEO. A company is known for its cutting-edge technology but has struggled with fostering a positive and inclusive workplace culture. The board of directors has recognized the need for a cultural transformation and appointed you, a dynamic and visionary leader, as the CEO.

You waste no time getting to work and initiating a comprehensive strategy. You understand that real change needs to come from within the organization, so you set out to empower and engage leaders at all levels. What might your first priority be? What else might you want to focus on? Following are some ideas.

First, you want to get out there in front of your people. This can include conducting a series of town hall meetings to communicate your vision for the company's culture. You emphasize the importance of collaboration, innovation, and a sense of belonging. You also make clear that this cultural shift would not be a top-down mandate but a collective effort that required the commitment of every employee.

In order to actively engage leaders, you can establish a leadership development initiative focused on empowering leaders. You want it to be designed to offer comprehensive training in emotional intelligence, effective communication, mentorship, and inclusive leadership.

You can encourage cross-functional collaboration initiatives that provide employees from different departments the opportunity to work together on projects that are outside of their usual responsibilities. This not only helps to break down silos but also encourages diversity of thought and perspective.

You can also make it clear that you have an open-door policy, and that any employee can email you or share their message anonymously through an online portal. This helps employees at all levels to share their thoughts, concerns, and innovative ideas without fear of retribution.

This is obviously a hypothetical situation with numerous variables. That's the beauty of it. It helps you be creative and let your imagination run loose. I've personally found scenario-based training similar to this to be extremely valuable—especially for people who have ambitions of leading cultural change.

Case Studies

I've always been interested in studying why some organizations rise to the top and others fail. Numerous organizations have embarked on transformative journeys, successfully breathing new life into their workplace cultures, demonstrating that substantial change is not only feasible but also within reach, while others have gone the way of the dodo bird. Here are a few organizations that have served as great case studies on the power of engaging and empowering people for sustainable cultural change:

- **Ford:** In the early 2000s, Ford faced financial difficulties and a reputation for hierarchical decision-making and resistance to innovation. In 2006 Alan Mulally, the former CEO of Boeing, was hired as the president and CEO of Ford. He implemented a cultural shift that encouraged transparency, collaboration, and a focus on teamwork. He emphasized open communication and accountability, which helped the company recover and regain its competitive edge. Ford was the only major US automaker to avoid bankruptcy during the financial recession in 2008–2009. Alan Mulally is known as the "Turnaround King."

- **Microsoft:** In 2013, Microsoft faced challenges in adapting to the mobile and cloud computing era, as competitors such as Apple and Google led the way. Microsoft's culture was seen as rigid and slow to innovate. Satya Nadella, as the new CEO, introduced a growth mindset and a more collaborative culture. He encouraged experimentation, embraced cross-functional teamwork, and shifted the focus toward cloud services and open-source collaboration. This cultural shift revitalized Microsoft's innovation and competitiveness.

- **IBM:** In the early 1990s, IBM was facing numerous financial challenges, and its culture was often described as bureaucratic and resistant to change. Under the leadership of CEO Lou Gerstner, IBM underwent a significant cultural transformation that focused on decentralization of decision-making, innovation, and a strong customer-centric focus. The company shifted from a product-centric approach to a solutions-oriented mindset, fostering a more dynamic and adaptive culture.

These examples highlight how effective leadership, strategic vision, and a commitment to cultural change can lead to successful turnarounds. In each case, the leaders recognized the need for a cultural shift, implemented strategic changes, and communicated a clear vision to inspire employees and stakeholders.

Shifting a Safety Culture

In 2017, Marathon Oil had a bad year safety-wise. At that time, Marathon was one of my clients, and I was providing a lot of leadership development training for their field supervisors. In January of 2018, their CEO, Lee Tillman, gathered leaders from all over the field and brought them to their corporate headquarters in Houston to put their heads together to figure out what was wrong and what they could do better. I helped facilitate this safety seminar and I watched as this Fortune 500 CEO got up to speak about safety. And I was amazed. He didn't just toe the company line and say what was expected of him as a CEO. Instead, he got up there and shed a few tears as he talked about the importance of safety and told a very personal story.

I watched how those in attendance responded and from there we created a three-hour safety leadership workshop unlike anything the organization had ever done before from a safety training standpoint. This workshop incorporated relevant discussions, out-of-your-seat activities, and practical tips around the ideas of service-based leadership and forward-looking accountability. The capstone of this workshop was something known as a safety stump speech, a brief yet personal story on why safety matters to you.

Telling stories in workshops is not anything new, and you'll often get one or two people who love to tell their story. But one challenge is that people talk in circles for eight or nine minutes without getting to the point, and everyone else mentally checks out. Their important message is lost. The safety stump speech we used at Marathon followed an easy three-part template that started with communicating your view on safety, moved on to your personal story or message, and wrapped up with your commitment. This template allowed participants to share their message in a very powerful and personal way. Some of the most powerful stump speeches I heard were 45–90 seconds long. Brief and personal.

We rolled these workshops out to every field-level employee and contractor at Marathon Oil. This is a heavily male-dominated industry. Many of these people work on oil rigs and are called roughnecks. They would come into the safety training, put their spit bottle on the table, and cross their arms. They didn't want to be there.

At the beginning of every workshop, I would share my personal safety stump speech and then I would tell everyone, "At the end of this workshop, each and every one of you will be getting up here right where I am and sharing your own story in front of everyone." You can imagine their lack of enthusiasm at the thought of being forced to stand up and talk. No one likes being made to speak in front of others unless you do it for a living like me.

But something amazing happened during this workshop because at the end these people were champing at the bit to get up and share their story. I saw some pretty tough people break down while sharing their story on why safety mattered to them and how they cared for everyone in that room. That is stuff that people will remember.

It was amazing, because some of the most powerful safety stump speeches that I heard had nothing directly to do with a work-related incident, but the moment someone starts saying words like son or daughter or tells a story about something people can easily relate to, they start to pay attention. Three weeks down the road we may not remember every single word, but we remember the key takeaways and how it made us feel.

Since 2017, Marathon Oil has seen a great reduction in their Total Recordable Incident Rate—a common safety metric. Of course, we could argue about how metrics are conducted and used until we're blue in the face, but the bottom line is that they've had fewer incidents, and fewer people have gotten hurt. We know the business case for being safe is there—it saves the company money—but more than that, it's the personal and moral obligation we have to look out for our colleagues.

This transformation of Marathon's safety culture did not happen overnight and did not happen through the workshops alone. It's taken a consistent effort by those employees that the senior leadership of Marathon Oil has engaged and empowered to make a difference. I'm honored to have played a small role in this, and I'm very proud of the work that we've accomplished.

Your Challenge

An important part of being able to empower others is both you and the other person recognizing what their strengths are. This challenge will not only enhance employee engagement by focusing on personal strengths but also empower individuals to take ownership of their professional development, fostering a positive and proactive work culture.

Here is what you need to do:

1. **Conduct a Strengths Assessment (60 minutes):**
   - Administer a strengths assessment tool. (I recommend Clifton StrengthsFinder, but you can use another reputable assessment.)
   - Discuss individual strengths profiles and what each strength means in the context of leadership and collaboration.

2. **Hold Interactive Discussions (30 minutes):**
   - Facilitate group discussions on how participants can apply their strengths in their current roles.
   - Share success stories of individuals or teams that have leveraged their strengths effectively.

3. **Embark on Action Planning (30 minutes):**
   - Guide participants in developing individual action plans for applying their strengths in their daily work.
   - Encourage them to set specific, measurable goals based on their newfound insights.

12

Making a Difference

Your journey through this book has woven through the threads of Leading Yourself, Leading Teams, and Leading the Culture. The topics we've covered and the experiences I've shared were carefully crafted to inspire and inform you as you continue your own leadership journey. In this final chapter, we'll reflect on these concepts and their transformative power in steering the course of leadership.

Part I: Leading Yourself

Leading yourself is the cornerstone of effective leadership. It requires self-awareness, discipline, and a commitment to personal growth. Leading yourself means cultivating a growth mindset, staying resilient in the face of challenges, and embracing a sense of purpose that guides your journey.

Chapter 1: Discover and Ignite Your Purpose

Your purpose is the unique intersection of what brings you joy, where your skills shine, and what the world needs—it's your journey, not your job. Igniting your purpose involves not only recognizing it but infusing it into every aspect of your life, transforming it from a dormant idea into a blazing source of motivation. I hope the experiences I shared of discovering and igniting my purpose inspire you on your journey.

Chapter 2: Embracing a Growth Mindset

A growth mindset is not merely a skill but a fundamental approach to challenges and opportunities. It is the lens through which we view setbacks not as failures but as stepping-stones to growth.

Embracing a growth mindset allows us a chance to learn, adapt, and evolve, ensuring a journey marked not only by personal success but by the lasting impact we make on the world around us. And remember, when faced with situations that trigger a high emotional reaction, don't forget to "wind the clock."

Chapter 3: Practicing Resilience

Resilience isn't about avoiding difficulties; it's about facing them head-on, armed with the belief that setbacks are not roadblocks but opportunities for growth. The adversity we face may be different, but I challenge you to continue to keep things in perspective and surround yourself with the right people. Our ability to be resilient is not just a personal asset; it's a beacon that inspires and uplifts those around us, fostering a culture of strength and perseverance.

Chapter 4: Continuous Improvement

The essence of continuous improvement lies in the commitment to refining processes, honing skills, and embracing a culture of learning. As you carry this momentum forward, please remember that improvement is an ever-unfolding journey—a testament to our resilience, adaptability, and unwavering dedication to becoming the best versions of ourselves. You can do great things, but you need to be proactive.

Part II: Leading Teams

Leading teams is a dynamic orchestration of being able to inspire others and lead through influence. Effective team leadership involves leading by example, active listening, and a commitment to cultivating a culture of trust and accountability. It's not merely about steering toward goals but empowering each team member to contribute their unique talents, creating synergy that propels the entire team toward success.

Chapter 5: Leading by Example

Leading by example is the foundational element of leading a high-performing team. It is a commitment to living in alignment with your values, demonstrating integrity, and exhibiting the qualities you expect from others. You set a standard of excellence through the consistent application of good leadership behaviors that makes you effective and inspires others to do the same.

Chapter 6: Service-Based Leadership

Service-based leadership transcends authority and prioritizes the well-being and growth of others. It is not defined by titles or hierarchical positions but by a commitment to uplift, support, and inspire. It involves developing authentic relationships, active listening, empathy, and a genuine dedication to the success of others.

Chapter 7: Motivating Others

Motivating others helps to ignite the spark within others, inspiring them to reach their full potential. Effective motivation is not a one-size-fits-all approach but a personalized and empathetic understanding of what drives each team member. It encompasses encouragement, recognition, and creating an environment where contributions are valued.

Chapter 8: The Art of Delegation

Delegation is not merely a transfer of tasks, but a thoughtful allocation of duties based on individuals' strengths and skills. It helps to enhance productivity, encourages autonomy, and cultivates a sense of ownership within the team while also providing opportunities for others to expand their skill set.

Part III: Leading the Culture

Leading the culture is a nuanced and impactful aspect of leadership that involves shaping the collective values, behaviors, and ethos of an organization. It goes beyond defining mission statements; it's about embodying the desired culture through actions and fostering an environment where those principles thrive. Leading the culture is not a passive role; it's an active, intentional engagement that sets the tone for organizational identity, cohesion, and long-term success.

Chapter 9: Creating a Culture of Accountability

Creating a culture of accountability is the bedrock of organizational success and helps to foster a collective commitment to excellence. Forward-looking accountability is not about pointing the finger at someone but rather an empowering force that encourages responsibility and continuous improvement. Leaders play a pivotal role in modeling accountability, showcasing that it is integral to growth and achievement. In cultivating this culture, organizations can adapt swiftly to challenges, learn from setbacks, and thrive through a shared commitment to taking ownership of actions and outcomes.

Chapter 10: Building a Positive Workplace Culture

Building a positive workplace culture is a transformative journey that goes beyond superficial perks, emphasizing shared values and genuine connections. A positive workplace culture involves recognizing and celebrating others, encouraging innovation, and creating an environment where individuals feel heard and valued. The result is not just a better work environment but a resilient and dynamic culture that propels teams to flourish, collaborate, and find fulfillment in their collective endeavors.

Chapter 11: Engaging and Empowering Others to Lead Cultural Change

Engaging and empowering others to lead cultural change is a dynamic process that involves inspiring a collective vision and fostering a sense of ownership within the team. Throughout this part of the book, we've understood that cultural change isn't a top-down directive but a collaborative effort where every individual contributes to the evolution.

Your Journey

As you continue on your leadership journey, remember to lead with purpose, inspire with passion, and leave an indelible mark. The journey is lifelong, filled with challenges and triumphs. Leadership is not a solitary summit but a collective ascent, and in embracing this path, my hope is that you will find fulfillment in the knowledge that your leadership has made a positive difference in the world. You stand not at an endpoint but at a new beginning, an open door to perpetual growth, endless possibilities, and an enduring legacy. Your impact can go far beyond individual achievements. It echoes in the growth of those you lead, the transformation of teams, and the evolution of organizational culture. As this final chapter closes, may you carry forward the torch of inspiration, igniting the potential in yourself and others.

Acknowledgments

I am humbled and grateful for the collective efforts and support that have contributed to this project coming to life. This has been so much more than just writing a book. It's been a transformative journey—one that started when I was a child—and I owe a debt of gratitude to those whose influence, guidance, and encouragement have helped shape the experience.

First and foremost, I extend my deepest appreciation to my beautiful wife, Shanna, for unwavering support and understanding throughout the process. Your encouragement has been a constant source of motivation. A big thank you to my four amazing daughters, Hazely, Haddie, Haven, and Harper. Being your dad is the greatest gift I could ever be given.

A heartfelt thank you to my fellow soldiers from "The Doghouse" and Sky Soldiers from the 173rd Airborne Brigade. Your insights have added depth and richness to the content of this book, and you've played a pivotal role in my own growth as a leader. I am privileged to have had the opportunity to serve with all of you.

Thank you to Leah Zarra at Wiley for believing in me and the value of my message. This book would not exist without you. And also to Kelly Talbot, my development editor, for your guidance and brilliance in making these pages come alive. Your attention to detail, constructive feedback, and commitment to excellence have transformed my ideas into a cohesive and impactful narrative. I appreciate the countless hours you've invested in refining and polishing this work.

Special recognition is reserved for the readers who embark on this leadership exploration. Your curiosity and commitment to personal and professional development inspired the creation of such content. I hope the insights shared in these pages serve as a source of guidance and inspiration on your own leadership journey.

Last, but certainly not least, I express gratitude to the countless leaders, past and present, whose stories and examples have shaped the landscape of leadership. Learning from your successes and challenges has been an enriching experience, and I am privileged to contribute to the ongoing conversation about effective leadership.

About the Author

Patrick Nelson has gained both local and national accolades for his military service, academic career, and work as a professional speaker and trainer, including being named the inaugural NFL-Tillman Military Scholar. He is an experienced leader who spent nearly seven years in the US Army as a paratrooper and completed three combat deployments leading soldiers. His military awards include the Bronze Star Medal and the Purple Heart Medal.

Patrick is an engaging facilitator who has conducted leadership development programs for a variety of clients, from Fortune 500 clients to small businesses and across a variety of industries. Off the proverbial leadership field, he serves his community by actively volunteering with Tee It Up for the Troops, a nonprofit organization that raises money for wounded veterans.

Patrick studied at Minnesota State University and received a bachelor's degree, graduating magna cum laude. He also has a master's degree in sport management from Minnesota State and a master's in organization development from Pepperdine University.

Index

199

Pulling security duty in April 2004 at an oil refinery outside of Kirkuk, Iraq. Note our lack of gun turret. We literally had to ratchet strap a tripod down on top of a Humvee – this is how we conducted all of our missions that deployment.

On my first deployment in northern Iraq in April, 2003.

With my friend and colleague Eddy Gonzalez in Afghanistan the summer of 2005. Eddy served his country for over 20 years and achieved the rank of Command Sergeant Major.

1st Platoon, Alpha Battery 4-319th AFAR at COP Keating in Afghanistan, June 2007.

On my last deployment to Afghanistan in March, 2008. We were getting ready to meet with local leaders to discuss border control operations.

Handing a Gatorade to small Afghan boy while working at Torkham Gate in Afghanistan in February, 2008.

Visiting with local kids in Afghanistan on my last deployment in the spring of 2008.

With my wife, Shanna, and our beautiful daughters in November, 2022.

My family in June 2023.

Our 4-H daughters sitting at the front door of the house we're building, late 2023.

Me in 2021 – soon after I embarked on my solo speaking career.

Speaking in Nashville, Tennessee, in April, 2021.

Our platoon in the spring of 2005 at FOB Shkin in eastern Afghanistan. Holding our guidon flag is Emmanuel Hernandez.

Chinook helicopter preparing to land at FOB Shkin in 2005 – the same landing zone the June 8 attack took place.

The Chinook helicopter that was resupplying us on June 8, 2005, when we came under a 107mm rocket attack.

Taken at the aid station soon after being wounded on June 8. To the right is my friend Landon Duff who was administering an IV to Damon Burnett.

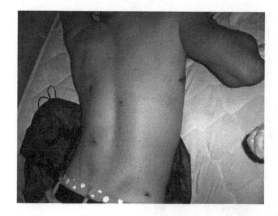

Wounds in my back from the rocket attack in Afghanistan.

Doctor checking the pulse on the leg of Damon Burnett after he was wounded in the rocket attack.

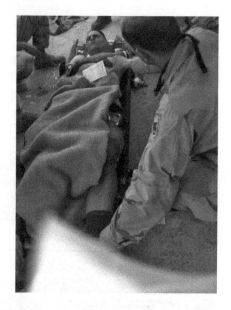

Myself, Joel Vega, and Jacky Shay Howard sharing a moment at the ramp ceremony as they loaded Emmanuel for his final trip home.

A picture of Emmanuel Hernandez from his memorial in Vicenza, Italy, in June of 2005.

My platoon leader Jon Post and I in March, 2005, as we prepared to leave Italy for Afghanistan.

Master Sergeant Greg Trent. Killed in Action August 8, 2012.

My friend and former Interpreter Ali Shah at Torkham Gate in Afghanistan, in the spring of 2008.

With my friend and former interpreter Ali Shah. I was honored to play a small role in helping him and his family flee Afghanistan in August 2021 as the Taliban took over.

My former interpreter and friend Ali Shah and his family as they prepared to embark on their dangerous journey to Kabul airport to leave Afghanistan.

My squad while operating at Torkham Gate in the spring of 2008.

My promotion to
Sergeant in 2004.

Being promoted to
Sergeant in 2004.
Pinning my rank on is
my friend and former
Commander Jacky
Shay Howard.

Observation Post Warheit in the summer of 2007. My home for 40 days.

With our interpreter Ray at Observation Post Warheit in the summer of 2007.

July 2007 at Observation Post Warheit. I got caught outside in a vicious downpour while investigating some small-arms fire one of the bases below us was receiving.

Picture taken at Observation Post Warheit in June, 2005. Behind me you can see the small landing zone where the infamous fuel blivit rolled down the mountain.

David Campbell and Chris Nemedez walking up the landing zone at Observation Post Warheit.

My challenge coin rack.

Joe Mauer and I at the 2013 MLB All-star game as part of the People Magazines Tribute to Heroes special.

With Admiral Mike Mullen at a Hope for the Warriors fundraiser in 2013.